WEDDING DAY
and Other Korean Plays

WEDDING DAY
and Other Korean Plays

Edited by
the Korean National Commission for
UNESCO

The Si-sa-yong-o-sa Publishers, Inc., Korea
Pace International Research, Inc., U.S.A.

Published simultaneously in KOREA and the UNITED STATES

KOREA EDITION
First printing 1983
The Si-sa-yong-o-sa Publishers, Inc.
5-3 Kwanchol-dong, Chongno-ku
Seoul 110, Korea

U.S. EDITION
First printing 1983
Pace International Research, Inc.
Tide Avenue, Falcon Cove
P.O. Box 51, Arch Cape
Oregon 97102, U.S.A.

ISBN: 0-89209-013-8

This book is a co-publication by The Si-sa-yong-o-sa Publishers, Inc.
and The International Communication Foundation.

Foreword

The Korean people are artistic, expressing their innermost being in pottery, painting, poetry, drama, music and dance. To most foreigners familiar with Chinese and Japanese art, Korean art comes as a profound revelation and a delightful experience. Korean art differs from the strong, bold aspects of continental Chinese art and from the dazzling colours of Japanese art. Its basic characteristic is simplicity, reinforced by the atmosphere of quiet and serenity which it creates.

Following the publication of *Modern Korean Short Stories*, the Korean National Commission for UNESCO embarked upon a new project, dedicated to seeking real character of Korean culture. This new series deals with various aspects of Korean culture—language, thought, fine arts, music, dance, theatre and cinema, etc. It concentrates on baring the roots of the Korean cultural tradition and demonstrating the process of its transformation. It is hoped in this way to reveal the framework of traditional thought which is fundamental to any understanding of Korea's past and present.

Profound thanks are due to the writers of the individual articles and to the generous sponsorship of the Si-sa-yong-o-sa Publishers, Inc., who once again have turned a dream into a reality. This series, edited by the Korean National Commission for UNESCO, is published by the Si-sa-yong-o-sa Publishers, Inc., in commemoration of the thirtieth anniversary of the Korean National Commission for UNESCO.

Bong Shik Park
Secretary-General
The Korean National Commission
for UNESCO

Contents

Introduction

Thé foreign reader interested in modern Korean drama has long awaited a translation of that medium into readable language. A prerequisite to understanding the present state of modern Korean drama is an acquaintance with the literature itself. Hence this collection of translations which gives a picture of the dramatic style and subject matter of Korean dramatists. The national character and the issues addressed in these works are of no minor consequence.

The plays compiled in this anthology, which have appeared from time to time in the *Korea Journal*, are not intended to represent a systematic review of Korean drama. Furthermore, this anthology is not a representative collection of the major works of the great number of playwrights who produced so prolifically in the years following the end of the Japanese domination of Korea in 1945. Considering the difficulty of introducing these works into English, which appear here in translation for the first time, this anthology can without doubt serve as a respectable guide to Korean modern drama.

The plays included in this volume are typical of the thirty year period from 1945 to 1975. Although only one work of each playwright is included, all of the writers, without exception, are able to speak with authority for Korean drama. The reader will no doubt find it easy to identify the way of handling the subject matter and the writing style insofar as these have been preserved in the translations. (It is always a legitimate question, though, to what extent the characteristics of the original are carried over through translation.) When speaking of dramatic tone, a subject which cannot be avoided in drama analysis, is the great diversity and individual character of each work, rather than their uniformity.

If the foreign reader is looking in addition for some aspect common to all of the works in this volume, one that can set modern Korean drama apart from others, it is the national character of the people. If at the same time, however, there are those who are hoping to find works that show no influence from Western thought but reflect instead a pure inheritance from a small country confined within an oriental tradition, it may be that these works appear to be "tainted" more or less by the Western style of dramaturgy. The truth of the matter is, the so-called new Korean drama, like that of her neighbors in Japan and China, has received a greater influence from modern Western thought than from their respective past traditions.

Let us take a closer look at the writers and their works in the order in which they appear in this collection. O Yŏng-jin's *Wedding Day* pictures the wedding customs practiced in a traditional society but in such a way that the humanness associated with the practice is touching. This legitimate comedy portrays in a humorous manner the contrasts between the genuine and the contrived, the arranged marriage and the love marriage. This kind of work contrasts greatly with the gloom and disillusionment of the realism which has tended to dominate modern Western drama. Anyone, however, can easily detect the irrationality of the repression exerted on human nature by the hierarchical Korean society which O Yŏng-jin has counteracted so well in a warm and humorous way.

This writer became well known for his satire and humor. In his later years and up until the time of his death in 1974 his pessimism became increasingly more apparent and could be said to have been the result of his disappointment with the realities of the period.

The next two writers, Ch'a Pŏm-sŏk and Yi Kŭn-sam, though there is a slight time lag between their initial debuts, both made their appearance in the period between the late

fifties and the early sixties. They are of the same generation and whereas their plays were produced in the same
modern setting their writing temperament is vastly different.
The first writer, Ch'a, observes the modern day world in a
realistic way and has a good eye for portraying what he sees.
Yi, by comparison, has an ability for caricature and intel-
lectualism.

"The Fourth Class Car" by Ch'a, is set in the period right
after 1950 when Korea was overrun by the invasion of the com-
munists from the north and the great majority of people were
compelled to live for a time in a very unsettled situation. This
is a relatively brief sketch of human relationships inside an
overcrowded railway car, but the writer's temperament and
ability for realism are comparatively well represented.

A New Common Sense on the contrary, exhibits the clever-
ness and ability of Yi to make fun of and ridicule in a way that
lends a light touch to his work. The utterly fantastic scenes in
which he displays his ability to handle the development of the
actors is one of the common characteristics of his works.

If Ch'a Pŏm-sŏk, Yi Kŭn-sam and O Yŏng-jin represent one
generation of dramatists, then the younger playwright, O
T'ae-sŏk can be said to belong to another generation. He began
to attract attention as a playwright from 1968 but his real
dramatic activity began in the seventies.

It was not only that his works represented the origin of individualistic expression in the drama medium, but this period
which became generally recognized as the era of new experi-
mental theatre saw O T'ae-sŏk as the leader of this new development.

Though his debut aroused no small stir in Korean drama
circles, the work introduced here is a very short piece and is
hardly adequate for an understanding of his entire production.
In this short one-character play, however, his distinctive
character is quite apparent. This playwright, rather than portraying the present state of life for the ordinary persons
through the slightly exaggerated, garrulous jesting of the

drug peddler, is more interested in exposing the irregularities and absurdities of the present-day world. It is likely that O T'ae-sŏk possesses that dramatic imaginative quality which can be the source of inspiration for an ever new and continuing production of dramatic works.

Yi Kang-baek made his debut in the early seventies as a very promising young playwright and gave the impression of possessing an inner treasure store of dramatic originality. He not only differs from his senior, O T'ae-sŏk, in the fairly transparent dramatic imagery, but also in his portrayal of reality. Now and then he also makes use of allegory. In addition, his exceedingly restrained literary style is in great contrast to the calculated loquacious style of O T'ae-sŏk, so that at times the risks in his formalizing are great. The one-act play "Getting Married" is an excellent example of the successful treatment of the dramatic clarity of his refined sensitivity.

The last work, *Wha. . .i, Whai, a Long Long Time Ago* by Ch'oe In-hun, displays a unique appeal in several aspects. To put it briefly, as far as drama is concerned, he was the first writer to include poetry as well as prose in his drama. His unique appeal is expressed in this firm belief that drama could be a form of poetry. He was convinced of the universal persuasive power of the dramatization of the archetypal fable. Also, that an elevated emotional feeling could be acquired through the economy and the omission, as far as possible, of language and movement. Ch'oe, too, made use of the intense dramatic metaphor in the etching of the subject matter of his drama.

The author endows this play which derives its dramatic motif from the universalized fable of the birth of a baby-to-be-a-hero with a strong local flavor, so much so that the reality of the work stands out very strongly. Despite the religious overtones of the work the accentuation of the tragic tone cannot escape notice.

Ch'oe first made his name as an intellectual and abstruse novelist. It was only in the seventies that, transformed into a dramatist, he sought his subject matter among the narrative history in the ordinary folk ways of the Korean people. It is not only his own contribution which is of importance but the impact he has made on drama in general.

Korean modern drama, exposed to Western realism and having grown up in its shadow, is in the process of trying to pursue its self-identity in this transitional period. While Ch'oe In-hun and other dramatists are extremely individualistic, they continue to make great achievements as dramatists of considerable original writing ability rooted in the Korean soil.

An in-depth study of a variety of Korean plays poses the question as to what is truly Korean. Perhaps this small volume can help provide some adequate answers to this question. It is hoped that this book will provide foreign readers with the opportunity to take an introductory look at Korean drama as it is.

Yoh Suk-kee

WEDDING DAY
and Other Korean Plays

Wedding Day

by O Yŏng-jin
translated by Song Yo-in

Characters

Mr. Maeng T'ae-ryang, a Yi dynasty civil servant holding
the title of Chinsa, i.e., one who has passed the first
examination
The Elder Maeng, his father
Maeng Hyo-wŏn, his uncle
Mrs. Maeng, his wife
Kap-pun, his daughter
The Ch'ambong, a junior official of the rear rank
The Wet Nurse
Ip-pun
Sam-dol, a valet
Kil-bo, a valet
Kim Myŏng-jŏng
Kim Mi-ŏn
Village Maidens (A and B)

1

Mr. Maeng's relatives (A,B,C, and D)
Tenant Farmers (A,B,C,D, and E)
Sedan-chair Bearers and Villagers

ACT I

Scene One

The action takes place at the respectable-looking guest room of Mr. Maeng T'ae-ryang's old-style house. On the left is the inner room, and a secluded meditation hall stands partially hidden in the rear. A tall fir tree stands in the corner to the right, towering over a thick growth of trees. As the curtain rises the stage remains vacant for a while. Mr. Maeng enters from stage left. He is excited and jubilant as he swaggers in.

Mr. Maeng: Anybody home? Isn't there anybody home? Don't you want to hear about my trip? Isn't there a soul awake in this house? (*A group of people enters from the inside.*)

Sam-dol: Yes, sir. I'm glad to see you back, sir.

Mr. Maeng: Listen, fellow, is the lady of the house in?

Sam-dol: Yes sir. In fact, she's quite anxious about the result of your trip, sir.

Mr. Maeng: Why be anxious? Go tell her to quit worrying and come out here right away.

(*Sam-dol exits inside. Kil-bo enters on a run, almost bumping against Sam-dol.*)

Kil-bo: Oh, I'm surprised you're back so soon, sir.

Mr. Maeng: I left Toraji-kol right after daybreak.

Kil-bo: Your father and the gentleman of Ŭnsan-kol are here, sir, to find out how things have worked out on your trip.

Mr. Maeng: The gentleman of Ŭnsan-kol? Oh, you mean my uncle is here, too? I'm not surprised.

Kil-bo: He's anxious to know what happened to that proposal while you were over there, sir.

Mr. Maeng: Are they all that anxious, really?

Kil-bo: Of course, sir. . . .

Mr. Maeng: They really don't need to worry. Go tell them I'll be with them right away.

Kil-bo: You mean it's almost as good as accepted, sir?

Mr. Maeng: Well, just remember who's been handling this deal.

Kil-bo: Certainly, sir. I told you so too, didn't I?

Mr. Maeng: Say, where's Kap-pun now?

Kil-bo: She's probably gone over to the hill in the back, digging up bellflower roots with Ip-pun and other girls from the neighborhood, sir.

Mr. Maeng: What? Dig up what? How thoughtless! Run after her and bring her back here right away.

Kil-bo: Yes, sir.

Mr. Maeng: She doesn't seem to care about what I'm going through for her sake. Imagine her being so thoughtless at a time when a decision is about to be made on whether she'll be able to marry that P'ansŏ *(board-president)* Kim's son or not! *(Mrs. Maeng and the Wet Nurse enter from the inside.)*

Mrs. Maeng: Dear, I hear you've come back with the proposal almost as good as accepted.

Mr. Maeng: Hello, darling.

Mrs. Maeng: I'd say it worked out just as beautifully as we'd expected, dear.

Mr. Maeng: Beautifully? *(Takes off his hat and gown proudly.)*

Mrs. Maeng: (Picking up the hat and gown and handing them over to the Wet Nurse) Now, tell me about the trip. How did it go?

Mr. Maeng: Well, I've got some surprises for you. The house has no less than one thousand square feet of room space set aside just for the servants. Just for the servants, do you hear?

The Wet Nurse: Oh, my goodness! One thousand square feet of room just for the servants—that's really fantastic,

Madam.

Mr. Maeng: And they've got barns that are full of grain and fruit of all kinds. Let me count them—one, two, three, four. . . .

Mrs. Maeng: It must be something like a royal palace, then.

Mr. Maeng: As a matter of fact, they treated me as cordially as if I'd been a guest from the royal palace.

The Wet Nurse: How nice! I just wish I could even take a look inside such a house. When Mistress Kap-pun goes to live in that house after her wedding, won't you please let me go along as her bridal escort, sir?

Mr. Maeng: Bridal escort? Certainly, nobody could be better qualified than the bride's wet nurse.

Mrs. Maeng: I'm afraid all this talk about escorting the bride and so on is a bit presumptuous, dear.

Mr. Maeng: Presumptuous? Remember who's been to that place. By the time I started out for Toraji-kol, I had everything figured out in my mind. I say I had everything figured out, and the chances for success had to be good, so I had confidence all along, ha ha. Nothing's really impossible, you know, darling.

Mrs. Maeng: Are you really telling me the truth? Did they really agree to our proposal?

Mr. Maeng: How could you possibly distrust me? Everything depends on a man's ability. I mean, a man's ability makes the whole difference. Ha ha.

Mrs. Maeng: I know you're a man of ability. Now, if this turns out to be a success we ought to commemorate your first major achievement in life by erecting a monument for you.

Mr. Maeng: A monument? I may even deserve it. . . .

Mrs. Maeng: It's no mean achievement, I tell you—it's just as tough as plucking a star out of the heavens.

Mr. Maeng: Look at me now, darling. From now on I'm an in-law of that influential P'ansŏ Kim. *(Shouting)* Say, nurse, will you go get Kap-pun and bring her over here right away?

The Wet Nurse: Yes, sir. *(Exits in a hurry.)*

Mrs. Maeng: After all, I think you really knew what you were doing when you bought that title of Chinsa. Of course, a title like that means no great honor these days, but still it's better than having no title at all.

Mr. Maeng: A bought title? Hush! Don't let anybody hear about it. You'll be wrecking my whole life if. . . .

Mrs. Maeng: That must be your father coming. *(Exits inside. Mr. Maeng's father enters with the help of the Ch'ambong Pak along with Maeng Hyo-wŏn. The Elder Maeng is a toothless wisp of a man, half in a dream.)*

Mr. Maeng: How have you been, Father? Oh, you've come from such a long distance, Uncle.

Hyo-wŏn: At a time when a great event is about to take place in the Maeng family, I couldn't possibly stay away from it, could I? *(Sits down on the verandah.)*

Mr. Maeng: *(Bowing to the elder Maengs)* I've just come back from Toraji-kol, sir.

Hyo-wŏn: How did you make out? Was the trip worth your effort?

Mr. Maeng: Yes, sir. I think it'll work out all right.

Hyo-wŏn: How? Did you get to meet P'ansŏ Kim?

Mr. Maeng: How could I miss seeing the man who's going to be my daughter's father-in-law?

Hyo-wŏn: So you met him, eh? How did it work out?

Mr. Maeng: How could anything go wrong when I personally set out to do it? Ha ha. I told them I'd give them the date on which to send us the four-pillar engagement note and the presents, after consulting with both of you.

Hyo-wŏn: Set the date already? When neither family has had a chance to meet the boy or the girl?

Mr. Maeng: Don't let that worry you, sir. They already know a lot about Kap-pun.

Hyo-wŏn: You're a skillful operator, indeed. But we've got to know a lot more about the boy, too. Did you get a good look at him?

Mr. Maeng: Oh, well, . . . it doesn't make any difference whether I met him or not, Uncle.

Hyo-wŏn: No difference? How silly can you get? You mean you went there to arrange a marriage, and yet didn't even meet the prospective bridegroom in person?

Mr. Maeng: He's got his family to prove he's all right. You don't have to worry about that, Uncle.

Hyo-wŏn: Nonsense! Is everything gold that glitters? If that's what you mean, you didn't even need to make that trip.

Mr. Maeng: I didn't think I should really try to meet him. I was afraid it might seem a breach of etiquette to that influential and prestigious family if I did. Furthermore, P'ansŏ Kim himself said. . . .

Hyo-wŏn: I don't agree with you. I've been told that Mi-ŏn, the bridegroom-to-be, is not an ordinary man.

Mr. Maeng: What do you mean by "not an ordinary man"? Has he got a harelip? Or is he one-eyed?

Hyo-wŏn: There's something terribly eccentric about him, they say.

Mr. Maeng: It's an eccentric boy rather than a normal, conforming one who has the potential of becoming a great man. Frankly speaking, we've got more faults on our side, sir. I mean, she's just the daughter of a Chinsa, whereas he's the son of a P'ansŏ. We might as well pick one with a clear edge over the others. It's no easy proposition to have that kind of influential family as our in-laws. For our own good in the future, you see, we need all the help they can give us. And, to be most frank with you, we've got nothing to lose but everything to gain from this match.

Hyo-wŏn: Something to gain? I don't like your idea. What do you think of it, my dear elder brother? The way he thinks. . .?

The Elder Maeng: Thinks of what? I can't hear a word of what you're saying. I've got mosquitoes in my ears. . . so all I can hear are the voices of some dead people calling me.

Hyo-wŏn: We're talking about T'ae-ryang's daughter Kap-pun. . . .

The Elder Maeng: Kap-pun?

Mr. Maeng: I mean your granddaughter. She's already eighteen, and it's about time we found a match for her. Don't you think so?

The Elder Maeng: Eighteen? Never thought she could be that old so soon.

Mr. Maeng: What do you think of her marrying P'ansŏ Kim's son?

The Elder Maeng: Who did you say?

Hyo-wŏn and Mr. Maeng: (In unison) The son of P'ansŏ Kim in Toraji-kol.

The Elder Maeng: P'ansŏ Kim of Toraji-kol? Good. P'ansŏ Kim is the one that was so smart as a child and passed the civil service exams when he was only fifteen, and then worked his way up to become a P'ansŏ at thirty. And his father was no ordinary man, either, and he enjoyed a pretty good life as Inspector of P'yŏng-an Province. To tell you the truth, it was money that made the elder Kim what he was, and his father was. . . .

Mr. Maeng: Father, I think we've got a pretty good match for her.

The Elder Maeng: A match? A match for who?

Hyo-wŏn: For Kap-pun, don't you hear?

The Elder Maeng: I see. But Kap-pun. . . who's she anyway?

Mr. Maeng: Oh dear, she's your granddaughter. It's my daughter Kap-pun, sir.

The Elder Maeng: I see.

Hyo-wŏn: What do you think of it, my dear elder brother? Do you approve of P'ansŏ Kim's son marrying our Kap-pun?

The Elder Maeng: Is Kap-pun going to marry P'ansŏ Kim? You couldn't have found a better match for her, but don't you think he's a bit too old for her?

Hyo-wŏn: I said P'ansŏ Kim's son, not P'ansŏ Kim himself.

The Elder Maeng: Well, well, I wonder whether P'ansŏ Kim

already has a grown-up son.

Hyo-wŏn: He certainly does. Don't you know?

Mr. Maeng: I think you're all confused, Father.

The Elder Maeng: All right, it's his son instead of P'ansŏ Kim himself. *(Sam-dol enters.)*

Sam-dol: Luncheon is ready, sir. Would you please help your father out to the dining room, sir?

Mr. Maeng: Won't you go over to the dining room, Father?

The Elder Maeng: Go where?

Hyo-wŏn: To the dining room for luncheon.

The Elder Maeng: (Rising with help) To the fortune-teller's? To find out if he's a good match for her?

Mr. Maeng: For luncheon, I said, not the fortune-teller's.

The Elder Maeng: I knew. We certainly need to have her fortune told to see if she's getting a good match. So go ahead and take off. I don't think I'll go along. Say, Sam-dol!

Sam-dol: Yes, sir.

The Elder Maeng: Don't just stand there like a totem pole. Hurry up and go fix my luncheon, will you? *(Stage light dim out.)*

Scene Two

The action takes place toward sunset a few months later. The Maeng brothers sit facing each other across a box of engagement gifts containing colorful satin and other dress materials, engagement rings, and accessories.

Hyo-wŏn: Why don't you answer me? Why? *(Pause)* These are nothing but humiliating gifts! I tell you it's not necessarily bad, especially when it has to do with a rich man's son marrying a poor man's daughter. But our family isn't all that poor. At least, not as poor as to accept that kind of gifts in return for our little daughter. We Maengs have, our own pride, standards of conduct and dignity, don't you know? *(Pause)* They didn't say anything about this kind of gifts when you were over there in Toraji-kol, did they?

Mr. Maeng: No, not at all, sir.

Hyo-wŏn: Really? If so, that's all the more reason you shouldn't have accepted the gifts in the first place. Just what made you accept them?

Mr. Maeng: I. . . I didn't think they were all that humiliating, sir.

Hyo-wŏn: What do you mean? You mean the gifts are a price you should be charging for the daughter you're selling off?

Mr. Maeng: Uncle. . . .

Hyo-wŏn: Strictly speaking, you're just selling your daughter. In other words, you're selling your daughter for the price of those gifts.

Mr. Maeng: You're being a little too harsh, Uncle.

Hyo-wŏn: No. If you still have any pride in your family, just send those gifts back to them.

Mr. Maeng: What you're saying is all very true, sir. But what would they think of us if we sent them back after all that time? I'm afraid it would mean a breach of courtesy to an influential and respectable family like theirs, and it would wreck the engagement we worked so hard to arrange, sir.

Hyo-wŏn: You talk about courtesy and manners all the time. Don't you think you ought to observe them just as much for your own family as for other people?

Mr. Maeng: (*Aggressively*) I want to make one thing clear to you, Uncle.

Hyo-wŏn: Go ahead.

Mr. Maeng: I'd thought all along that by getting into an in-law relationship with them we might be able to enhance our own standing and also get some help from them as we went along. . . .

Hyo-wŏn: That doesn't make any sense. Are you corrupt enough to feel greedy for that kind of influence?

Mr. Maeng: What's wrong with having some influence? What am I doing wrong by trying to raise the prestige of our own family, Uncle?

Hyo-wŏn: That's enough! *(Jumping to his feet)* How could we enhance our own standing after accepting that kind of humiliating gifts? You're a fool not to realize that kind of gifts simply ruins our reputation. You do what you like. But I warn you not to be a maverick in the family. And don't do anything to make our family a laughingstock. I won't tolerate it. Now I've got to be on my way.

Mr. Maeng: Let me tell you something, Uncle.

Hyo-wŏn: I don't want to talk about it any more, and I don't want to hear your flimsy excuses, either. If you really must talk to me, come over to Ŭnsan-kol. *(Exits to the guest room.)*

Mr. Maeng: He's being terribly pigheaded! What's wrong with what I'm doing? I'm doing whatever I like with my own daughter, and he can't butt in like that just because he's my uncle! What's the matter with him, anyway?

Mrs. Maeng: Oh, why don't you talk to him in person if you've really got something to say, dear? You're talking to yourself like a puppy barking at the moon.

Mr. Maeng: You just don't know what's going on here. Say, darling, am I not supposed to receive things like that?

Mrs. Maeng: What do you mean?

Mr. Maeng: Would you say those gifts are humiliating to us?

Mrs. Maeng: Those gifts? What does it matter if people say they're humiliating gifts? After all, gifts can always come and go.

Mr. Maeng: Exactly, but that uncle of mine has been harassing me like mad because of them. I just can't put up with his ways.

Mrs. Maeng: You shouldn't get excited like that, because you're already familiar with his ways. You really shouldn't be quarreling on a happy day like this, dear.

Mr. Maeng: I didn't start it. He told me to return those engagement gifts right away. Don't you think it's a problem?

Mrs. Maeng: Happy events attract many devils. I suppose that

Uncle was merely being jealous. But if Kap-pun finds out about it, she'll get hysterical, and cry like mad. So would you calm down and collect yourself for her sake?

Mr. Maeng: Since when has that little daughter of mine been all that serious about her marriage? Tell me.

Mrs. Maeng: You'll be surprised to hear this. When the four-pillar note arrived a while ago to formalize the engagement, she was clinging to the door eavesdropping on us all the time. She must know she's getting a good match. You see, girls these days are quite different.

Mr. Maeng: Ha ha. So there's some truth in the proverb that says, "Daughters are arrogant thieves." *(Kap-pun enters.)* Our own daughter is interested in nothing but running away from us.

Kap-pun: I'm not interested in running away from you, Father.

Mr. Maeng: Listen, were you clinging to the door eavesdropping on us when the note came?

Kap-pun: Impossible! I didn't, Father.

Mrs. Maeng: Don't tell me you didn't.

Kap-pun: You must have told him everything, Mother. I'm embarrassed.

Mrs. Maeng: Embarrassed? You're a shrewd one.

Mr. Maeng: Soon you'll be a daughter-in-law of P'ansŏ Kim. You should be careful about your manners. You shouldn't run around, playing with snivelling little girls of the village. And you should stop playing with maidservants like Ip-pun.

Mrs. Maeng: I think Ip-pun's all right, because she's been with you all the time, practically growing up together.

Mr. Maeng: Servants are servants, no matter what. Your mother doesn't care enough about manners. No wonder you're so pitifully ignorant of manners when the wedding's to take place any time now.

Kap-pun: Ip-pun has been crying and whining these past few days, asking me to let her come with me.

Mr. Maeng: What? Who comes with you where? It was my

uncle who gave me a hard time this morning, and now it seems to be the maidservant's turn. *(To Ip-pun as she enters.)* Listen, Ip-pun, you just can't go away with her! It's not proper! *(Exits to the guest room.)*

Ip-pun: Miss, how come you cheat me like that?

Kap-pun: What did I cheat you out of?

Ip-pun: You told me to wait just a minute and then you sneaked away without me. Isn't that cheating?

Kap-pun: When did I. . .?

Ip-pun: You see, the way you're acting now, you won't even bother to look at me with half an eye on the day of your wedding. *(Looking at the gifts)* Oh my, how beautiful and dazzling they are! Why don't you try them on, Miss?

Mrs. Maeng: Ip-pun, watch your language, won't you? Don't play with her from now on, because she's not a friend of yours any more. She's going to be a daughter-in-law of an important man. Remember that.

Ip-pun: I'm well aware of that, Madam, but aren't these all made of gold?

Mrs. Maeng: Don't touch them any more!

Mr. Maeng: (Off) Kap-pun!

Mrs. Maeng: That's your father calling you, Kap-pun. *(Kap-pun exits.)*

Ip-pun: I'd like to go along with her and do whatever I can to help her there. I'll do everything exactly the way she tells me to, Madam. I really want to go along, Madam.

Mrs. Maeng: You're out of your mind to say such a thing. Think of what your master might say if he heard you.

Ip-pun: Then how can I live in this lonely house after she's gone? *(Becoming tearful)*

Mrs. Maeng: I know how you must feel, because you two have grown up together, suckling at the same breast. But then, you're a maidservant and she's your mistress. Furthermore, her in-laws are no ordinary people. Your poor manners there, may simply disgrace this family... no, don't let me hear that again. *(Pause)* I'll be filling the place of your mother, and Sam-dol will take the place of your mistress. *(Pause)* (I'll buy you a house and you can marry Sam-dol and live like Kap-pun, talking about the good old days together. Won't you agree?

Ip-pun: I don't like Sam-dol, Madam. I like one person like Mistress Kap-pun better than ten people like Sam-dol.

Mrs. Maeng: You're being stubborn.

Ip-pun: I just can't live without my mistress Kap-pun. I'll go along with her.

Mrs. Maeng: So you're not going to listen to my advice! You'll regret this, do you hear? *(Exits, carrying the gift box. Sam-dol enters.)*

Sam-dol: Ip-pun! Why are you crying? Is it because you're sad about your mistress going away after she gets married? Or are you just jealous? You don't need to be so jealous, I tell you. You just wait a little while. Do you understand?

Ip-pun: (Drawing back) Go away!

Sam-dol: (Drawing closer to her) Humph, I won't!

Ip-pun: (Drawing back again) Why won't you? Why?

Sam-dol: You know why. Didn't you hear the madam saying the other day that you and I were to be. . . ?

Ip-pun: I'm not interested.

Sam-dol: Why not?

Ip-pun: Because you're lying!

Sam-dol: I'm not lying, Ip-pun. *(Two Maidens, A and B, enter.)*

Maiden A: Well, when a mullet cuts a splash so does a globe-fish, too.

Maiden B: When are you going to get married, Ip-pun?

Ip-pun: Shut up! Who said I'm getting married?

Maiden A: You're stuck up because you're going to be a maidservant to the daughter-in-law of an important man.

Maiden B: (To Sam-dol) Say, Ip-pun's bridegroom, won't you go over and bring Mistress Kap-pun out here?

Sam-dol: Stop joking, will you? *(Exits.)*

Maiden A: Here she is. Look at that Kap-pun, the bride I

mean. She's quite stylish the way she walks now.

Maiden B: You look splendid, Kap-pun. *(Kap-pun enters.)*

Kap-pun: Hello, girls!

Maiden A: Well!

Maiden B: Aren't you going to throw a party for us?

Kap-pun: What kind of party?

Maiden A: Don't try to fool us. We saw that messenger leaving your house after delivering the engagement note.

Kap-pun: It's something that'll happen to all of you, too—not just to me alone.

Maiden B: But you're awfully lucky to be engaged to. . . .

Maiden A: Someone in P'ansō Kim's family. . . a high-ranking official, you know.

Maiden B: How lucky you are!

Maiden A: When is the wedding day?

Ip-pun: The date hasn't been set yet.

Maiden A: I hear it'll be pretty soon, though. *(Kap-pun nods her agreement.)*

Maiden B: How nice! We're going to be invited to have lots of wedding cake and noodles before long, aren't we?

Maiden A: I hear your fiancé is an outstanding man. He's really a good-looking man, isn't he? *(Kap-pun nods.)*

Maiden B: He can write as beautifully as Su Tung-po, can't he? *(Kap-pun nods.)*

Maiden A: He's as good at calligraphy as Wang Hūi-ji, isn't he? *(Kap-pun smiles.)*

Maiden B: *(Clapping her hands)* See, it looks as though we've already met him. *(The two Maidens keep badgering Kap-pun.)*

Kap-pun: Leave me alone, will you?

Ip-pun: Leave my dear mistress alone, you ill-mannered girls!

Maiden A: What did you say? You sound as if we were taking her to pieces or something.

Maiden B: *(To Ip-pun)* Just how much social standing do you think you have yourself? You ought to watch your language, do you hear?

Ip-pun: Listen! Go away, both of you! Miss!

Kap-pun: Yes? What can I do for you?

Ip-pun: You know what, Miss. Won't you take me along with you?

Kap-pun: I'm not in a position to do anything about that. My parents should have an idea on that.

Maiden A: Oh, my goodness, she's asking her to take her along and live together with the in-laws.

Maiden B: What are you going to do with Sam-dol?

Ip-pun: If you take me there, I'll do everything according to the rules.

Kap-pun: That's enough! Go back to work and don't let my mother catch you saying that. *(Ip-pun exits toward the back of the house, dejected.)*

Mr. Maeng: (Carrying a book of his family history) Kap-pun!

Maidens A and B: How are you, sir?

Mr. Maeng: (Ignores the greeting.) How many times do I have to tell you? Get back in there right this minute! *(Kap-pun exits.)* Now, girls, don't come to my house any more. From now on Kap-pun is no friend of yours, do you understand? *(The Maidens exits, pouting.)*

Mr. Maeng: Ha ha. I'm an in-law of P'ansŏ Kim—and my daughter is the eldest daughter-in-law of that family. You poor little girls have no business coming to my house now. You girls have no manners. *(Swaggers into the room jubilantly.)* Ch'ambong! Ch'ambong!

The Ch'ambong: (Off) Yes, sir.

Mr. Maeng: What's keeping you so long?

The Ch'ambong: (Entering, carrying a writing brush and a piece of paper) I've been grinding some writing ink, sir.

Mr. Maeng: Come on over here and open it up for me.

The Ch'ambong: Yes, sir.

Mr. Maeng: What a dull family history it is. I see nobody has ever gotten to be anything important in the last several generations. . . until I became a *Chinsa* in the present generation. And yet my uncle gives me a hard time like that. . . do you understand what I mean, Ch'ambong?

The Ch'ambong: I certainly do, sir.

Mr. Maeng: You know I'm getting my daughter married off to a P'ansŏ's son, don't you?

The Ch'ambong: Oh yes, I certainly do, sir.

Mr. Maeng: Now go ahead and write it in. Kap-pun, the eldest daughter of T'ae-ryang, marries Mi-ŏn, the eldest son of P'ansŏ Kim Ch'i-jŏng. No, let's put it this way. The son-in-law of Chinsa T'ae-ryang was Mi-ŏn, the eldest son of P'ansŏ Kim Ch'i-jŏng.

The Ch'ambong: It makes no difference one way or the other, sir.

Mr. Maeng: Beg your pardon?

The Ch'ambong: Oh, it's nothing, sir. I'll write it in large, conspicuous letters. *(Ip-pun is seen setting up a bowl of pure water in the back yard and offering a prayer to it.)*

Ip-pun: Holy Spirit, I never thought my mistress Kap-pun would ignore my wish like that. I'm all by myself with no parents or relatives. Mistress Kap-pun and I grew up together and I came to depend on her just like a real sister. I can't live without her. I'll be too lonesome without her. Please let me go along with her. Please, Holy Spirit. . . . *(A youth, looking like a Confucian scholar, who has been watching Ip-pun praying, steps in from behind the house.)*

Youth: Young lady. . . .

Ip-pun: Oh, my goodness!

Youth: I'm just a traveler passing through.

Ip-pun: There are menservants in the guest room if you go out there.

Youth: Oh, I'm sorry for this intrusion. I didn't know I was in the ladies' section of the house. *(Exits.)*

Mr. Maeng: Didn't you hear someone out there, Ch'ambong?

The Ch'ambong: Well, it's too late for anyone to drop in for a visit, sir. Your uncle was walking away all excited and angry, saying he'd never set foot here again. *(Ip-pun runs into the inner room.)*

Mr. Maeng: Stop running around the house, Ip-pun, and go in there and help them out, will you? *(Kil-bo enters from the great room.)*

Kil-bo: Sir, it's a student of Chinese classics. He's asking us to put him up for a couple of days.

Mr. Maeng: Put him up? My house is not a bird's-nest. And my guest room is already full. So why don't you tell him to try some place else?

Kil-bo: Yes, sir, I will. *(Exits.)*

Mr. Maeng: Oh, what a bad day I've been having since day-break today! *(Climbing onto the verandah)* Let me read it. *(In a chanting tone)* Maeng So-and-so had a son of *Chinsa* rank named T'ae-ryang, whose eldest daughter was named Kap-pun, whose husband was Mi-ŏn, the eldest son of P'anso Kim Ch'i-jŏng. . . Mm. . . I should take this over to my uncle and surprise him. Would that terrible uncle of mine still put me down?

The Ch'ambong: Your family history is now very colorful, sir.

Kil-bo: *(Re-entering)* I've sent him away, sir.

Mr. Maeng: Well done. If we let him stay with us out of sympathy, he would simply eat up our food and we'd have nothing to gain. What's a roving Confucian scholar good for in this day and age?

The Ch'ambong: He must be in a messy situation to go begging around like that.

Kil-bo: But then as he was being shown his way out, he said he'd have a hard time trying to reach Toraji-kol before dark.

Mr. Maeng: Listen, you fool! Did he really say he lives in Toraji-kol?

Kil-bo: Yes, he did, sir. But why do you ask that, sir?

Mr. Maeng: Why do I ask that? You fool! Don't you know Toraji-kol is where P'ansŏ Kim lives?

Kil-bo: I certainly do, sir.

Mr. Maeng: Listen, get out there and bring him back, will you? I'm afraid we've made a big mistake.

Kil-bo: I don't know what to make of this.

Mr. Maeng: Where are you, Ch'ambong?

The Ch'ambong: Here, sir.

Mr. Maeng: Oh, get busy and bring them here, will you?

The Ch'ambong: Bring what here, sir?

Mr. Maeng: My hat and gown, do you hear?

The Ch'ambong: (Circling) Your hat and gown?

Mr. Maeng: Don't you know where they are?

The Ch'ambong: I do, sir, but you're in an awful hurry. Well, the hat is. . . .

Mr. Maeng: Hurry up and throw that gown over on me! .

The Ch'ambong: Yes, sir. But you don't have to be in such a hurry, sir. The hat is. . . .

Mr. Maeng: Why should I not be in a hurry? A slight slip-up on my part may wreck the whole thing! *(Kil-bo and Kim Myŏng-jŏng enter.)*

Mr. Maeng: (Fondling the hat as he steps down toward the guest) I must apologize to you for our rudeness a while ago. I hear you're from Toraji-kol, and the fools in my house didn't even tell me about your coming from there. So we were rather rude to you.

Kim Myŏng-jŏng: May I ask who you are, sir?

Mr. Maeng: Certainly. I'm Maeng T'ae-ryang, the master of this house.

Kim Myŏng-jŏng: Is that right, sir? I'm sorry for this intrusion. I'm Kim Myŏng-jŏng, a student of Confucian studies, living in Toraji-kol. As I said a while ago, I thought I would ask you to put me up for a day or two as I wanted to see your meditation hall which, I hear, is well built and nice and quiet.

Mr. Maeng: No trouble at all, sir. The hall may be a bit less inviting than people realize, but it's a solid building. I hope you'll just relax and spend one or two months with us. . . well, won't you have a seat over here please? *(Both sit down facing each other.)*

Kim Myŏng-jŏng: I hope I'm not imposing on you, sir.

Mr. Maeng: Not at all, sir. Since you're from Toraji-kol, do you happen to know Taegam Kim Ch'i-jong?

Kim Myong-jong: Taegam Kim Ch'i-jong? Oh, you mean P'ansŏ Kim?

Mr. Maeng: Yes, that's correct, sir.

Kim Myŏng-jŏng: Who wouldn't know P'ansŏ Kim, who's so powerful and influential as to be able to bring down a bird in the sky? I know him quite well, sir.

Mr. Maeng: Oh, you do. You see, he's going to be my daughter's father-in-law.

Kim Myŏng-jŏng: So I seé. A very happy event indeed. Congratulations, sir!

Mr. Maeng: Thank you, sir. I think they're meant for each other with Heaven's blessing. Now, if you're ready you can come over and take a look at the meditation hall.

Kim Myŏng-jŏng: Thank you, sir.

Mr. Maeng: Ch'ambong! Kil-bo! Go in there and tell them we have a guest from Toraji-kol and so. . . you haven't had dinner yet, have you?

Kim Myŏng-jŏng: Not yet, sir. I'll be much obliged if you give me just a little something to eat. Am I not imposing on you too much, though?

Mr. Maeng: No, not at all, sir. You're quite welcome. Listen, hurry up and fix a hot meal, and then. . . .

Kim Myŏng-jŏng: If you have anything left over, that'll be quite all right for me. Please don't bother to have another meal prepared just for me, sir.

Mr. Maeng: I couldn't serve anything left over to a welcome guest from Toraji-kol. You see, it all depends on what kind of guest you have. And don't forget to bring some wine and appetizers on another tray. Never mind. I'll go fix up the drinks myself. But you had better bring some water for our guest to take a footbath in. *(Exits inside.)*

Kil-bo: (Bringing in a footbath and washes the guest's feet) You might have gotten into trouble trying to reach Toraji-kol before dark, if we hadn't stopped you, sir.

Kim Myŏng-jŏng: Your master is a virtuous man—he'll be blessed with a lot of happiness. By the way, why did he pick P'ansŏ Kim's son, of all people, as his son-in-law?

Kil-bo: What do you mean by "of all people"? The eminent son of P'ansŏ Kim can write as beautifully as Su Tung-po and is as good at calligraphy as Wang Hūi-ji, and he's as good-looking as any man can be. He's just about perfect. Why do you say "of all people," sir?

Kim Myŏng-jŏng: Your description is quite accurate except for his looks.

Kil-bo: Except for his looks? Do you know him well?

Kim Myŏng-jŏng: I certainly do. In fact, he and I are bosom friends. I'd thought he wouldn't be able to find a match for himself, and would probably have to lead a lonesome life the rest of his life. But he was indeed lucky to be engaged to the wonderful daughter of this family. You must realize that there was something wrong with him since, though the son of a ranking official, he couldn't find a girl to marry him until he was well past twenty.

Kil-bo: Something wrong?

Kim Myŏng-jŏng: Blossoms have come out on a dead tree, so to speak.

Kil-bo: Blossoms come out on a dead tree? Do you mean the fiancé is in no shape to get married?

Kim Myŏng-jŏng: There's one thing wrong with him that's worse than being one-eyed or harelipped.

Kil-bo: What could that be?

Kim Myŏng-jŏng: (*Drying his feet*) It's this. (*Into Kil-bo's ear*) He was born a cripple.

Kil-bo: (*Dumbfounded, mimics a cripple.*) Oh, good heavens, this is going to make a lot of people unhappy. Sir! Sir! (*Runs inside whispering to the Ch'ambong, who is petrified, disappearing behind the room. Mr. Maeng enters on the run, all excited, and goes over to Kim Myŏng-jŏng.*)

Mr. Maeng: Say, my friend from Toraji-kol (*Mimicking a cripple*), did you say he's like this?

Scene Three

The setting is the same as before. The Maengs are having an emergency family meeting. Their voices break the gloomy silence of the room.

Relative A: It's too good a family to give up.

Relative B: She's too precious a child to give away.

Relative C: We can't give one or take the other—we're in a real predicament.

Relative A: The problem is, one of his legs is a bit longer than the other.

Relative B: In other words, one of the legs is a bit shorter than the other.

Relative C: Heavens, it's quite a problem now. He was born a cripple, and now he's over twenty with all his bones grown stiff and hard. So there's no way of curing him at all.

Relative A: Even Confucius said we should stay away from that kind of cripple.

Relative B: And he's not just lame. He's an awful-looking cripple.

Hyo-wŏn: We've got a big problem to solve—let's be a bit more serious about it.

Relative C: It's a pity T'ae-ryang didn't meet the boy in the first place when he went over there.

Relative D: Meet the boy? Why, he certainly should have done that. How could he skip that in such an important matchmaking deal?

Hyo-wŏn: You're right. I myself insisted on it at the very beginning. But he just kept saying that it would mean a breach of etiquette to such a distinguished family. Where the devil are you, T'ae-ryang?

Relative A: Take it easy! You can have all the good intentions in the world and still end up like that. Remember that to err is human.

Relative B: It's no use crying over spilt milk. So let's see if we can think of any way out of this predicament.

Hyo-wŏn: Any way out? We're just stuck, and there can't be any way out of it. Do you have the magic power of lengthening the short leg or shortening the long one?

Relative A: This is no time to blow your top. (*Mr. Maeng and the Ch'ambong enter, unconcernedly.*)

Hyo-wŏn: His calculations were all wrong. You know what he said? He said, "what have we got to lose by becoming an in-law of P'ansŏ Kim?" "We've got nothing to lose but a lot to gain from such a relationship in the future." Didn't you say so? Remember now, you're responsible for all this. Wise men have cautioned us against coveting material gains in matchmaking, don't you know?

Mr. Maeng: You're being a bit too harsh and unfair, Uncle.

Hyo-wŏn: Shut up that big mouth of yours! Nobody will listen to you.

Relative A: None of us have anything to be proud of. Let's be a little quieter.

Relative B: Certainly. Now, what's done is done. Our task today is to find some clever and effective way of solving this problem. We could go ahead with the wedding as planned, as if nothing had happened. But then our Kap-pun won't go along, judging by the way she's protesting now.

The Ch'ambong: You want to know something? She was thoroughly upset, saying, "A cripple, you say—who's going to marry him? For the life of me, I won't. Not me!"

Relative B: We feel sorry for the one directly involved, but what really matters is the dignity of the Maeng family. After all, it's a promise made by a *yangban* family to another *yangban* family, and so. . . .

Relative A: Why don't we break it up?

Relative D: Break it up? I hear they're ready to come over and get her any time now. How could we justify breaking it up at this stage?

Relative B: We couldn't do that now, because we haven't even met the boy in person.

Relative C: It was our own fault skipping that procedure in the first place.

Relative B: Isn't there some clever way out of this?

Relative C: You see, we're holding a tiger by the tail.

The Elder Maeng: (Snores, blissfully ignorant of what is happening.)

Hyo-wŏn: Like father, like son. *(Rises to leave.)*

Relative C: Let's go home; we're hungry too.

Relative A: We're not going to get anywhere sitting here like this. *(Hyo-wŏn and the four Relatives exit.)*

Mr. Maeng: If you're all leaving, what shall I do all by myself? Ch'ambong!

The Ch'ambong: Yes, sir.

Mr. Maeng: (Pacing up and down nervously) Isn't there any way we can get out of this mess?

The Ch'ambong: I wish I knew, sir.

Mr. Maeng: You're no better than I am. I mean your brain's no better than mine. Move over, will you? I want to speak to Father about it. Father! *(Squatting in front of him unobtrusively)* Father, we're in trouble, Father. . . .

The Elder Maeng: (Talking bosh) Ah, I'm falling asleep. I fall asleep all the time. Ha. *(An innocent smile spreads on his face.)*

Mr. Maeng: Father, they say Mi-ŏn is a cripple.

The Elder Maeng: What?

Mr. Maeng: I said Kap-pun's fiancé is a cripple. What shall we do? It's a gentlemen's agreement between the two *yangban* families. So we can't break it up. Nor can we go ahead with the wedding. What shall we do to get out of this mess? I wonder if you have any good idea, Father. Do you? Father?

The Elder Maeng: What are you talking about? You chatter like a dying man and I can't make anything out of it, Son.

Mr. Maeng: I said Mi-ŏn is a cripple, Father.

The Elder Maeng: My own? You mean my own meal is ready now?

Mr. Maeng: I said "Mi-ŏn," not "my own."

The Elder Maeng: Mi-ŏn? Oh, Mi-ŏn. . . let me see. . . who can that be?

Mr. Maeng: Mi-ŏn is Kap-pun's fiancé, Father. And Mi-ŏn is. . . *(In a hysterical tone and mimicking a cripple)*. . . like this. He's a helpless cripple, like this. What shall we do? What can we do?

The Elder Maeng: (Wearing a blissful smile and wetting his lips) A great many years ago an old man named Lao Lai-tse put on children's colorful holiday clothes and bounced around like a little boy asking his father to catch some sparrows for him. His father, who was one hundred years old, was very happy to see his son acting that way. Ha ha. Are you trying to bounce around like that Lao Lai-tse? Children are children to their parents, even if they're one hundred years old. I'm pleased with you, Son. But that's enough for now. Ha ha.

Mr. Maeng: This is no time to be talking about Lao Lai-tse, Father. *(In a frantic tone)* Mi-ŏn is a cripple!

The Elder Maeng: Who is a cripple?

Mr. Maeng: It's Mi-ŏn, the fiancé of Kap-pun's.

The Elder Maeng: Kap-pun? I see. Her wedding's set for tomorrow, isn't it?

Mr. Maeng: Good Heavens! Mi-ŏn is a. . . . *(Kim Myŏng-jŏng enters, all dressed up and ready to leave.)*

The Ch'ambong: Hush!

Mr. Maeng: What's up now? *(Spots Kim and motions the Ch'ambong and his father to exit.)*

The Elder Maeng: You want me to go back to my room? Then bring my clothes over there. I'd never expected to see her wedding while I was alive. Ha ha. *(Exits with the Ch'ambong.)*

Mr. Maeng: I see you're all dressed up. Are you leaving now?

Kim Myŏng-jŏng: I'm much obliged to you for your hospitality, sir. I must go back home now and I'm here to say good-bye to you.

Mr. Maeng: Then you're going back to Toraji-kol?

Kim Myŏng-jŏng: Yes, I am. By the way, what was the matter this morning? I heard people crying and arguing.

Mr. Maeng: Oh, nothing. It was just a bunch of tenant farmers arguing about some petty problems. They got a bit too noisy, so I sent them away.

Kim Myŏng-jŏng: Really? The tenant farmers? They're always a nuisance. Ha ha. Well, I must be on my way. If you have any message for your in-laws there, I'll be happy to deliver it for you.

Mr. Maeng: Oh, no, thank you. We're just impatiently waiting for the wedding day—my daughter, the fiancée, and myself, the father-in-law-to-be. She said. . . .

Kim Myŏng-jŏng: Does the fiancee have a problem, sir?

Mr. Maeng: No, not at all. She is quite happy, but a bit worried, though. She says, "I'm not sure if I could do everything to the satisfaction of my husband's family."

Kim Myŏng-jŏng: Is that right, sir? I suppose a lot of things could keep a girl's mind busy before her wedding day.

Mr. Maeng: By the way. . . .

Kim Myŏng-jŏng: By the way. . . .

Mr. Maeng: About that fiancé of my daughter's. . . is it true that he is a. . . ?

Kim Myŏng-jŏng: Oh, the rumor has hit your place, too. Well, it couldn't have started out of nothing. . . it could be quite true.

Mr. Maeng: Which leg is it anyway? Do you know which one's out of shape?

Kim Myŏng-jŏng: I see you're a little unsettled with the wedding coming up so soon. Ha ha. *(Exits.)*

Mr. Maeng: (Almost in tears) After all, it wasn't just a bad dream or a joke, but it is a fact! Say, my friend from Toraji-kol. . . . *(Exits in a hurry following Kim Kap-pun enters, stamping her feet on the floor, followed by Mrs.*

Maeng and Ip-pun.)

Kap-pun: Dear me, oh dear. . . I'm just sick of it all!

Mrs. Maeng: I'm sorry, Kap-pun. Will you come over here and listen to me? I know how terrible you must feel about it. But it's an agreement with a *yangban*. So what shall we do, Kap-pun? Won't you think it over, please?

Kap-pun: Ip-pun! Why don't you take my place, if you really don't mind it?

Ip-pun: How could you say that, Miss?

Mrs. Maeng: You shouldn't say that sort of thing to your own mother, Kap-pun. Once upon a time there lived. . . .

Kap-pun: Once upon a time there lived what? You're talking about that large snake again—the story of a girl marrying a large snake to be filial to her parents, and then ending up wealthy and all that. Just what are you taking me for, Mother?

Mrs. Maeng: You're my only child and I don't mean to let you down. The problem is, we've already set the date and now you're balking like that—what shall we do?

Kap-pun: I'm sick of it all. If you really insist on it, I'll just kill myself, Mother.

Mrs. Maeng: Don't say that! Oh, my goodness, I'm quite out of luck!

The Wet Nurse: (Off) Madam, would you please come over and check the rice cake and meat slices?

Mrs. Maeng: You just go ahead and prepare them the way you like. . . I'm busy. Since we've already started it, I guess we might as well bake some rice cake and cut some meat slices. *(Comes across Maidens A and B on her way out.)* Hello, girls!

Maiden A: How are you, Mrs. Maeng?

Maiden B: Do you mind if we drop in for a visit?

Mrs. Maeng: No, not at all. Come right in. Kap-pun feels so sad to think of having to part with you girls. *(Exits. The Maidens look saddened.)*

Maiden B: Listen, Kap-pun. Don't wear your heart out,

because it's something that just can't be helped.

Maiden A: You're looking pale and skinny.

Kap-pun: Who is? Of all things!

Maiden B: We're really sorry about that, Kap-pun. Isn't one of his legs supposed to be longer than the other?

Maiden A: No, they say one is shorter than the other. He's supposed to have been born a cripple, isn't he?

Kap-pun: Leave me alone, Girls.

Maiden B: Let's not talk about it. Wouldn't you be mad, too, if you were in her place?

Maiden A: I certainly would. Besides, she's even made baby things well in advance of the wedding.

Maiden B: And she's always been puffed up. Wouldn't even give us a decent look.

Maiden A: (*Mimicking a cripple*) Your sweet darling will be limping like this when he goes out.

Maiden B: He'll be limping like that when he comes back home, too. (*Ip-pun enters, watching the girls ruefully.*)

Ip-pun: You nasty little girls! You're just making it worse. Get out of here! Go away!

Maiden B: You're mad because he's limping like this, eh? (*The Maidens exit, limping and giggling.*)

Ip-pun: Please don't pay attention to those ill-bread girls, Miss. And you shouldn't be worrying so much. I'm really worried about you. It almost breaks my heart. (*Sobs.*) You ought to pull yourself together, Miss.

Kap-pun: Pull myself together? You don't have to worry about me like that. I'm all right. I'm perfectly all right.

Ip-pun: No. I know what I'm talking about. You look all right on the outside, but you're different inside. Your mind is full of dark clouds. I know it.

Kap-pun: Never mind. Everything'll be all right if I just don't get married.

Ip-pun: Oh my, you don't mean that, do you? That's impossible. You couldn't make that kind of decision just because of that. No, you couldn't.

Kap-pun: What do you mean by "just because of that?" You mean I should go ahead and marry that miserable cripple? Would you do that if you were in my place? Tell me what I really should do.

Ip-pun: Of course, you should marry him.

Kap-pun: The very idea!

Ip-pun: It doesn't matter whether it's a harelip or a cripple.

Kap-pun: (In a rage) Then what do you think really matters?

Ip-pun: True love. If there's true love, I don't think anything else matters.

Kap-pun: True love? Oh, you're talking about love.

Ip-pun: I'm sure your fiancē is full of true love for you. And that's what really matters.

Kap-pun: (Crying) How can you be so sure? Have you been married to him?

Ip-pun: Oh, my goodness! *(Mr. Maeng enters.)*

Kap-pun: You go ahead and marry that cripple if you like him so much, and live with that true love the rest of your life! I won't stop you!

Mr. Maeng: (Slapping his knee as if with a revelation) That's an idea!

Kap-pun: Father!

Mr. Maeng: (Drawing back in surprise) Yes, what is it? You're driving me to my wit's end.

Kap-pun: You're an unmitigated fool! *(Exits inside.)*

Mr. Maeng: Pardon?

Ip-pun: I'm so sorry for you, Miss. *(Exits quickly.)*

Mr. Maeng: (To himself, merrily) Don't worry about it, Kap-pun. I'm not so heartless as to force you to marry a cripple. And I'm not going to break up this marriage, either. You just wait and see. Nothing's really impossible where I set out to do something. It's an absolutely brilliant idea, you see. Ch'ambong! *(The Ch'ambong enters.)*

The Ch'ambong: Yes, sir.

Mr. Maeng: Go get me the Sedan-chair Bearers, will you?

The Ch'ambong: Sedan-chair Bearers, sir? You have plenty of time even if you call them on the day of the wedding.

Mr. Maeng: You don't know what I'm going to do now. *(Whispers to the Ch'ambong.)*

The Ch'ambong: Heavens, I hope it will work out all right. If only it works out!

Mr. Maeng: Don't you worry about it! I've got everything figured out in my mind. Not even a Zhuge Liang can outwit me in this.

The Ch'ambong: I understand. It's a splendid idea, indeed. Say, Kil-bo! Sam-dol!

Mr. Maeng: Don't call them. I want you to go get them yourself. We shouldn't let any of our servants know about this idea. And tell Mrs. Maeng and the nurse to come out here, too.

The Ch'ambong: Yes, sir. I'll go get them. *(Exits as Sam-dol enters.)*

Sam-dol: Were you looking for me, sir?

Mr. Maeng: No, I wasn't. Oh, it's you. You've been working very hard these past few days and nights. Here, take this and go get drunk and have fun. I've got to fix you up with a pretty bride one of these days. Just don't worry about it, and I'll find you a charming match. Do you understand?

Sam-bol: (Giggles.) Then would you let me go ahead and marry Ip-pun soon?

Mr. Maeng: Why do you stick to Ip-pun alone? There's Kŭmnye, Kop-tan, and T'an-sil—they're all yours to choose from.

Sam-dol: Still, I prefer Ip-pun, sir. She's a bit aloof and you can't get close to her. When she's cross her eyes scare you. . . and she's sharp all around. You don't know much about her. That little girl is. . . .

Mr. Maeng: That's enough, and now get out of here!

Sam-dol: Where shall I go, sir?

Mr. Maeng: Hurry up and go get drunk!

Sam-dol: Yes, sir. *(Exits.)* I just don't understand that old skinflint giving me money and yelling at me to go get drunk. *(Kil-bo and Mrs. Maeng enter.)*

Kil-bo: Would you go in there and see what's happening, sir? I'm afraid something's going to happen to our mistress Kap-pun.

Mrs. Maeng: Darling, what shall we do now?

The Wet Nurse: Our mistress is beginning to look strange, as if she were out of her mind.

Mr. Maeng: Hush! Be quiet please. Listen, Kil-bo! Here, take this.

Kil-bo: Oh, it's money—thank you, sir, but. . . .

Mr. Maeng: It's not enough to take care of your wedding, but you can buy your engagement gifts with it in the future.

Kil-bo: Oh, you're being so generous, sir. *(To himself)* I wonder what's happened to that old skinflint.

Mr. Maeng: *(In a low, serious tone)* Listen, Kil-bo, I want you to go after Sam-dol and get him drunk and have him stay away for a few days. Make sure he doesn't set foot in here during that time. Do you understand?

Kil-bo: Why, what's the matter with Sam-dol, sir?

Mr. Maeng: It's none of your business. You just do what I tell you to. Now hurry up and go!

Kil-bo: Yes, sir. *(Exits.)* I just don't understand all this.

Mr. Maeng: That ought to take care of that end. Ha ha. Everything on earth depends on how smart and capable you are. Ha ha.

Mrs. Maeng: My goodness, you sound so confident, when she's threatening to kill herself—I just don't understand what you're up to, dear.

Mr. Maeng: Well, you're not foolish enough to believe that I'm going to let our daughter, the only child we've got, marry that cripple, are you?

Mrs. Maeng: If there's any way out of it, we'll be most fortunate.

Mr. Maeng: You want to know if I've found such a way, don't you?

Mrs. Maeng: Yes, have you?

Mr. Maeng: I certainly have, darling. This is where my tact and ability come in. Listen to me carefully. *(Whispers into her ear.)*

The Wet Nurse: Oh my, isn't that something. . . .

Mr. Maeng: "Splendid" again—is that all you can say about it? Now, hurry up and get Kap-pun ready to leave and bring her out here.

Mrs. Maeng: Nurse! *(The Wet Nurse nods and exits.)* I want you to go along, too.

The Wet Nurse: (Off) Certainly, Madam.

Mr. Maeng: It's your ability and nothing but your ability, ha ha. . . *(On this line enters the Ch'ambong followed by Sedan-chair Bearers.)* Oh, you're all here.

The Ch'ambong: Yes, sir.

Mrs. Maeng: I wonder what's taking Kap-pun so long to get ready. *(Exits in a hurry.)*

Mr. Maeng: Do you know where Ŭnsan-kol is?

Sedan-chair Bearers: Yes, we do, sir.

Mr. Maeng: Do you know where the house of Maeng Ch'osi is in Ŭnsan-kol?

Sedan-chair Bearers: We certainly do, sir. *(The Wet Nurse, Mrs. Maeng and Kap-pun enter.)*

Mrs. Maeng: You know the whole story, don't you, Kap-pun? Take care of yourself and goodbye!

Mr. Maeng: You couldn't harass your father any more now, Kap-pun.

Kap-pun: Father! Mother!

Mrs. Maeng: Yes, Kap-pun. Just tell the grandmother in Ŭnsan-kol that your father has sent you over.

Mr. Maeng: Nurse, you take it easy and stay with her until we send for you. I'll speak to my uncle about all this.

The Wet Nurse: Goodbye now. *(Ip-pun enters on the run.)*

Ip-pun: Oh my, aren't you going to tell me where you're going, Miss? Oh, no. I've got to go with you. You can't go anywhere without me, Miss.

The Wet Nurse: Stop nagging and behave yourself, will you?

Ip-pun: (Clinging to Kap-pun) No, you can't do this to me—
not saying anything about it to me. You have no pity.
You can't go away without me, Miss!

Kap-pun: Ip-pun!

Mr. Maeng: Now, take off, you Sedan-chair Bearers. *(The
Sedan-chair Bearers exit.)*

Ip-pun: Take me with you, Miss! *(Follows the Sedan-chair
out.)*

The Wet Nurse: You stay back here, Ip-pun! *(Exits after Ip-
pun. Maeng Hyo-wŏn enters.)*

Hyo-wŏn: What's happened?

Mr. Maeng: I've just sent Kap-pun over to your house to hide
there for a while, sir.

Hyo-wŏn: Good.

Mr. Maeng: Won't you come on over to the verandah, sir?

The Ch'ambong: Please come on up, all of you, sir. *(The
group goes up on the verandah.)*

Hyo-wŏn: Now, the problem is that maidservant of ours.
Will she do as we tell her? Won't that be rather difficult?

Mr. Maeng: We'll have to do the best we can. The confounded
cripple will come rushing in the first thing in the morning,
and we'll have to make do with any substitute bride that's
available. Sure, it'll be difficult, but we'll have to do it by
hook or by crook.

Hyo-wŏn: I agree with you. But suppose her parents or relatives find out about it. Wouldn't they give us a lot of trouble, saying that we've wheedled her into marrying a cripple, taking advantage of her being a lowly maidservant?

The Ch'ambong: Fortunately, though, she hasn't got any
parents, brothers or sisters, or any relatives whatsoever.

Hyo-wŏn: That takes care of it nicely.

Mr. Maeng: And she would be less than human if she didn't
realize how much she's indebted to us for having brought
her up ever since she was a little child. If she turns out
ungrateful and balks, then we'd have to force her to. . . .

Hyo-wŏn: No, you should talk her around. It's better to make it work by talking her around. (*Exits.*)

Mrs. Maeng: Where are you, Ip-pun? Everybody's waiting for you. Will you come out here for a minute?

Ip-pun: Yes, Madam. What's up anyway? (*Looks around.*)

Mrs. Maeng: Won't you come over here, Ip-pun?

The Ch'ambong: Will you go up there just for a minute? (*Helps her get up on the verandah.*)

Mr. Maeng: Ip-pun.

Ip-pun: Yes, sir.

Mr. Maeng: Listen, Ip-pun, from today on you're no longer Ip-pun. Do you understand?

Ip-pun: Pardon me, sir?

Mr. Maeng: You're going to be Kap-pun. You've taken over her place.

Ip-pun: Pardon me, sir?

Mr. Maeng: My daughter Kap-pun won't be around for a while, at least officially.

Ip-pun: Oh my, you make me scared.

Mr. Maeng: I wish you'd do as I say.

Ip-pun: No, sir, I won't. If Mistress Kap-pun has disappeared somewhere, then I'll disappear, too. If she has died, then I'm going to die, too.

Mr. Maeng: I'm pleased you're as loyal as all that to your mistress.

Ip-pun: I don't think I'll be able to live without her even for a day, sir.

The Ch'ambong: Isn't she commendable?

Mrs. Maeng: She certainly is.

Mr. Maeng: Then you're ready to do anything—positively anything—that Kap-pun tells you to do, are you not?

Ip-pun: Yes, sir, I'll do anything. I can even be cut in ten pieces if that's what she wants me to do.

The Ch'ambong: Isn't she commendable?

Mrs. Maeng: She certainly is.

Mr. Maeng: Then will you take the place of Kap-pun and marry that cripple in Toraji-kol?

Ip-pun: Pardon me, sir? Marry that cripple in Toraji-kol? That's something I couldn't possibly do, sir.

Mrs. Maeng: We're not joking, Ip-pun.

Ip-pun: No, Madam. I can do anything but that. It's not fair.

Mr. Maeng: Even if that's what Kap-pun wants you to do?

Ip-pun: Yes, sir. I just couldn't do that. I could kill myself if that's what she wants me to do. But I just couldn't bring myself to. . . .

Mr. Maeng: You're shrewd. You've been lying to me all this time about how loyal you are to Kap-pun. Your deeds don't match your words.

Ip-pun: Oh, my God!

Mr. Maeng: You're being ungrateful to us after all we have done to bring you up for the past twenty years.

The Ch'ambong: Think it over, Ip-pun. You've got nothing to lose.

Mrs. Maeng: That's true. And a bumpkin like Sam-dol can't hold a candle to that man. His leg might be a bit so and so, but then you'd be a daughter-in-law of that powerful official. (*Sam-dol has been eavesdropping for a while after entering in a thoroughly drunken mood.*)

Sam-dol: Sir! A bumpkin like Sam-dol? A boy Ch'un-hyang is better even if he's a cripple? How can you say things like that? You're breaking your promise! Your promise to me!

Mr. Maeng: Look at that fellow, Ch'ambong! How did he manage to sneak back here?

The Ch'ambong: Listen to me, boy! What happened to your manners?

Sam-dol: Ip-pun, you're a fool. You ought to know better than sit in on this kind of talk so nice and quiet! Haven't you got sense enough to realize you can't go to Toraji-kol as a substitute bride? Don't you fear Heaven? How can a maid-servant like you keep your status secret and win the confidence of that respectable person? No, Heaven forbid it!

The Ch'ambong: Listen to me, boy! If you're drunk, there are better ways to be drunk than that. And that's positively no way to behave in the presence of your master.

Mr. Maeng: Where's Kil-bo anyway? He must be out of his mind—I told him clearly enough! *(Kil-bo enters, thoroughly drunk.)*

Kil-bo: You've sneaked away—just like a mouse! You rascal! When did it happen? Come on, you rascal, let's go!

Sam-dol: Jealous of my strong legs? Why do you keep tracking me down and bothering me all the time? Damn it! Get out of my way!

Mr. Maeng: Listen, Kil-bo. Are you trying to give me a hard time, too?

Kil-bo: No, sir. I guess I just had one too many and that's why I'm in this terrible shape. Sam-dol saw an oxcart passing by the wineshop, and that made him think of coming to see Ip-pun, so he just sneaked out of the place without my knowing about it, sir.

Mr. Maeng: What a way to disgrace my family! Won't somebody throw them out?

Kil-bo: Say, Sam-dol, let's get out. You better change your mind about Ip-pun. She's no good any more. Let's go get drunk some more. Now, come on!

Sam-dol: Shut up! Isn't Kap-pun my girl? My master has made it very clear that she's going to be mine. Why don't you answer me? Is it all right for a master to betray his servant by double talk? I tell you, a master who cheats and takes advantage of his servant has gone to the dogs no matter how noble a *yangban* he may be.

The Ch'ambong: Stop it!

Sam-dol: He's gone to the dogs, hasn't he?

Mr. Maeng: Ch'ambong, will you take care of this fellow for me?

The Ch'ambong: Kil-bo, come over here.

Kil-bo: Sam-dol, it's all fouled up. Come over here, you fool. *(The Ch'ambong and Kil-bo drag Sam-dol out.)*

Sam-dol: You just wait and see, sir. I'm going to break the news so the whole village will be in an uproar. Ip-pun, he's

broken his promise. Broken his promise to me! *(Maeng
Hyo-wŏn enters.)*

Mr. Maeng: A ruffian like that should be dealt with roughly.
What a detestable fellow he is!

Hyo-wŏn: Why are you making such a fuss with the servants,
T'ae-ryang?

Mrs. Maeng: Ip-pun, here comes my brother-in-law. We
women might as well make ourselves scarce. *(Exits.)*

Mr. Maeng: Uncle, we've solved this problem once and for all.

Hyo-wŏn: How? What kind of mischief are you up to?

Mr. Maeng: Look at that girl over there. Doesn't she look
quite charming and courteous? From today on she's going
to be just like my own daughter. Ha ha. You see, everything depends on your ability. You just don't inherit it
straight from Zhuge Liang. What does it matter if my son-
in-law is a harelip or a cripple? Ha ha. *(Hyo-wŏn looks
disgusted, but Mr. Maeng is visibly pleased.)*

ACT II

Scene One

The action takes place two or three days later. The setting is
the same as that for Act I. On the verandah and in the room
are things to be used at the wedding ceremony, including
foods and decorations. The Ch'ambong mounted on a stool, is
addressing a group of tenant farmers in the yard.

The Ch'ambong: In other words, due to unavoidable circumstances Ip-pun, whom you all know well, has taken the
place of Kap-pun. That is, Ip-pun is now Kap-pun and
Kap-pun is. . . Kap-pun herself.

Tenant Farmer A: (Rising) Then which one's getting married?

The Ch'ambong: Of course, Kap-pun is going to be the daughter-in-law of P'anso Kim.

Tenant Farmer A: Then it's Kap-pun who's getting married.

The Ch'ambong: Wait, no, no. Which Kap-pun do you mean?

Tenant Farmer B: Aren't you saying that Ip-pun has become Kap-pun and Kap-pun has become Ip-pun?

The Ch'ambong: Beg your pardon?

Tenant Farmer C: You've got it all mixed up. Now, if we go by what you've just told us, the one who's getting married is Kap-pun. But as a matter of fact, it's Ip-pun that's getting married. If so, just what happens to the Kap-pun that's not getting married?

The Ch'ambong: Wait, let's take it up one by one.

Tenant Farmer D: It's all so complicated I can hardly follow it.

Tenant Farmer E: (Squatting down, explaining the relationship to Tenant Farmer D, perhaps most logically, by using three pieces of straw) It's not complicated. I'll solve it by arithmatic. This one is Ip-pun and she has become Kap-pun. *(Puts two pieces of straw together.)* The two have become one, haven't they? Now, of the two, one has to get married. . . so this \one \goes. *(Separates one piece a good distance away.)* But the one that's going to get married is none other than this Kap-pun, do you understand?

Tenant Farmer D: So what happens to the one that stays?

Tenant Farmer E: One that stays?

Tenant Farmer D: Is it Ip-pun or Kap-pun?

Tenant Farmer E: If I split that one I'll get fractions, Ch'ambong. *(Stands up, raising both hands in despair.)* Why should anyone make things so complicated in the first place?

The Ch'ambong: You still don't understand it, eh? Listen to me carefully. I'll go over it again for you.

Tenant Farmer D: (Rising) I know it. I know it. In other words, Ip-pun is like a tenant farmer, whereas Kap-pun is like the landholder, isn't that right? It's all that simple.

Tenant Farmer A: You just don't know what you're talking about.

Tenant Farmer D: And why do you say that? In other words, isn't it true that it's us tenant farmers who till the soil and grow crops, but it's the landholder who reaps the harvest? Let's apply the same principle here—the daughter-in-law of P'ansŏ Kim is going to be Kap-pun, whereas the one who's getting married is Ip-pun—isn't Ip-pun the tenant farmer and Kap-pun the landholder in this case?

Tenant Farmer C: That sounds good. But I still don't understand the case of the Kap-pun who's *not* getting married.
   (Mr. Maeng enters and listens.)

Mr. Maeng: Would you move over, Ch'ambong? *(Climbing to the stool)* Don't rack your muddled brains to figure it out. I'm saying this again. We'll hold the ceremony very soon, and I want all of you to pay no attention to who the bride turns out to be. Do you understand? If you by any chance slip up and say, "Good heavens, the bride is Ip-pun!" or "What's happening here?" after the bridegroom and his party have come in, somebody on that side will hear it and we'll be in trouble. So be careful about it and keep your mouths closed, do you understand?

The Group: Yes, sir.

Tenant Farmer D: We haven't done anything to let our master down ever since we can remember, sir.

Mr. Maeng: Now, you may leave except for those of you helping with the chores.

Tenant Farmer A: You never know what you'll run into in this world.

Tenant Farmer B: It sure beats me. *(The Tenant Farmers exit, splitting toward stage right and left.)*

Mr. Maeng: Damn it, I've had to go through all that trouble just because of Sam-dol. He spread the word around in all these villages, and I haven't seen him since this morning. I wonder where he is. Ch'ambong, I want you to make sure no one makes any trouble after the bridegroom's party has come in.

The Ch'ambong: Don't worry about it, sir.

Mr. Maeng: I hope you won't let me down. By the way, what kind of noise is that? *(The Ballad of Toraji is heard from far away.)* Great heavens, it sounds like the bridegroom's already.

The Ch'ambong: No, sir, it couldn't be the bridegroom's party yet. At least not this soon. . . .

Mr. Maeng: Oh, isn't it? I'm just nervous at the thought of meeting that cripple.

The Ch'ambong: You must take it easy, sir.

Mr. Maeng: How's the bride coming along with her make-up and so on?

The Ch'ambong: Don't worry about that, sir. She's been prettied up in good time. Her face has been powdered, her cheeks rouged, her hair combed, and she's put on a jacket with rainbow-striped sleeves and a pendant trinket on top of that. She now looks as pretty as a swallow fresh out of a bath, and as charming as the rising half-moon. . . a girl like Kap-pun can't even begin to compare with her— maybe not exactly so—but she does look totally different, though.

Mr. Maeng: Ip-pun looks totally different? Tell her to come out here so I can see her.

The Ch'ambong: Yes, sir. *(Sam-dol staggers in as he starts to exit.)* Sam-dol!

Mr. Maeng: Come on, you fool! Is this any way to behave in front of your master?

Sam-dol: No, sir. I was going to kill myself—only I ended up hurting my leg. (Stretches his legs, sitting down.) I kept drinking till I thought I would die of it, but in vain. So I jumped into the river, only to be saved by people fishing nearby. Then I tried to hang myself on a tree, but there wasn't anybody around to stop me and I couldn't bring myself to die like that. *(Rising, gazing at the feast table in front of the verandah)* Ip-pun, you senseless wench! Are you really going away? Look, I may be a lowly servant but I'm strong and healthy. Does that crippled son of a *yangban* still appeal to you? You cheap wench! I feel like wrecking your marriage, Ip-pun!

Mr. Maeng: I'm going to kill you, you bastard! *(Goes at him.)*

Sam-dol: Humph! Are you trying to hit me? Go ahead and hit me. But then I can pass just one word along to P'ansŏ Kim and this marriage is going to be wrecked!

The Ch'ambong: (Pushing Mr. Maeng aside) Listen to me, Sam-dol. Take it easy, will you? I'll get you any girl you like if you forget Ip-pun, I promise. If you like Kop-tan, I'll get her to marry you.

Sam-dol: No, thanks.

The Ch'ambong: Then how about Kŭm-nye? She's beautiful, witty, graceful, sharp, sweet. . . .

Sam-dol: No, thanks!

The Ch'ambong: Then who is it you like? Tell me. Tell me which girl you like, will you?

Sam-dol: It's no one else but Ip-pun.

The Ch'ambong: Stop being so stubborn. . . you're so incooperative, you're pigheaded. Come on, stop being that way and. . . .

Sam-dol: Did you say "pigheaded"? And who deserves being called that more? If you really mean to get me a girl to marry, please let me have your Kap-pun.

Mr. Maeng: Oh, you fool!

The Ch'ambong: You want to have Kap-pun? Are you out of your mind?

Sam-dol: Why should that surprise you? It is all the same thing. Ip-pun has become Kap-pun and Kap-pun has become Ip-pun. It doesn't make any difference one way or the other, do you understand?

Mr. Maeng: (Infuriated) You ignorant bastard!

Sam-dol: If you don't like the idea, just forget about it. *(Rises.)*

The Ch'ambong: Say, Sam-dol.

Mr. Maeng: Leave him alone! Ch'ambong, I'm going to teach that bastard a lesson. *(Kil-bo re-enters panting for breath.)*

Kil-bo: Sir, the bridegroom seems to be getting close. The mounted procession is headed toward the village entrance now.

Mr. Maeng: They sure keep their word, reaching here just at the peep of dawn. How diligent the cripple is! Kil-bo, go in there and have Ip-pun and her mother. . . Sam-dol, aren't you going to go get drunk? Together with Kil-bo?

Sam-dol: How can I go get drunk when I've got mountains of work to do? I've got to get out there to meet the bridegroom, and before the whole thing breaks up I might as well tip the bridegroom off.

Mr. Maeng: Well, I guess you win—you're right.

Sam-dol: Does that mean you're going to let me have Kap-pun, sir?

Mr. Maeng: Let you have Kap-pun? Damn it, bastard!

Sam-dol: Then. . . . *(Rises.)*

Mr. Maeng: All right, all right! I'll let you have her. You just help me out in this. I'll give you everything. Now you go back in there. Here, take this money! *(Kil-bo takes the money and exits with Sam-dol behind him.)*

Kil-bo: Listen, Sam-dol, you've got it made.

The Ch'ambong: Sir, how could you possibly make that kind of promise to him?

Mr. Maeng: Whew! *(Wiping sweat)* What have I done wrong in my former existence to go through all this? By the way, Ch'ambong, stop worrying and go over there and keep an eye on them, will you?

The Ch'ambong: Yes, sir. *(Exits in a hurry.)*

Mr. Maeng: Whew! *(The Wet Nurse enters with Ip-pun, who has been prettied up as a bride, and a few steps behind her enters Mrs. Maeng.)*

The Wet Nurse: Sir?

Mr. Maeng: Good Lord!

The Wet Nurse: Just take a look at our bride, sir.

Mrs. Maeng: What do you think of her, dear?

Mr. Maeng: Well, she looks completely different. Hush! *(Muzzles his mouth in a hurry.)* She's really a beauty. Our Ip-pun, hush, that is, our Kap-pun is a real beauty.

The Wet Nurse: Now we should hurry up and teach her the ceremonial procedures, Madam.

Mrs. Maeng: Go ahead and teach them to her. *(Womenfolk enter from the verandah. Servants keep coming and going. The bridegroom's party is heard approaching still closer.)*

Mr. Maeng: Oh, he's really coming now, Ip-pun, I mean Kap-pun! The bridegroom's coming. Remember what I told you—once you go there to live with your in-laws you should first of all take good care of your parents-in-law, and especially try to be on good terms with your mother-in-law. Not only should you observe the manners and etiquette to the best of your ability, but you must also do your very best not to debase the Maeng family in any way. Do you understand? *(Ip-pun doesn't answer.)*

Mr. Maeng: Why don't you answer me?

Mrs. Maeng: You shouldn't act that way.

The Wet Nurse: Please say "yes, sir," Kap-pun.

Ip-pun: (Choked up) Yes.

Mr. Maeng: That doesn't sound correct. Say "yes, sir!"

The Wet Nurse: Not just "yes" but a loud and clear "yes, sir!"

Ip-pun: Yes, sir.

Mrs. Maeng: Etiquette is quite rigidly observed over there, so you should be particularly careful.

Ip-pun: Yes, Madam.

Mr. Maeng: You still don't sound correct enough the way you say "Yes, Madam."

Ip-pun: Yes, Madam! *(Cries bitterly.)*

Mrs. Maeng: Just what makes you cry like that?

Mr. Maeng: And listen to me, Ip-pun, oh bless my memory, Kap-pun. . . you should never for a moment forget that you're my real daughter! Do you understand? *(The bride-*

groom's party is heard yet closer.)

Mr. Maeng: Oh, they're getting awfully close now.

Mrs. Maeng: Listen, don't forget to call me "Mother" now.
You'll be ruining the whole thing if you call me "Madam."
Do you understand?

Mr. Maeng: Well, let's give it a try, Ip-pun, oh God, I'm slipping again, Kap-pun I mean! Well, just try calling me
"Father!" Go ahead.

Mrs. Maeng: And now go ahead and call me "Mother," will
you?

The Wet Nurse: Come on, say it, Kap-pun. *(The bridgroom's
party gets still closer.)*

Mrs. Maeng: They must have arrived now. *(The Ch'ambong
rushes in.)*

Mr. Maeng: Come on, let's give it a quick try Ip-, er. . .
Kap-pun!

Ip-pun: Father!

Mrs. Maeng: Now try it on me.

Ip-pun: Mother! *(Collapses in tears. Mr. Maeng exits to the
guest room.)*

Mrs. Maeng: You've done well. Now, just don't forget to do
everything as you've been told to. Do you understand?

The Wet Nurse: Come now. *(Wiping tears off Ip-pun's face.)*
The wedding day for a woman is supposed to be the
first blossoming in her life, and anyone who cries on that
day naturally makes her life an unhappy one. So just
don't be that way, Kap-pun. *(Exits to the inner room
together with Ip-pun. The ringing of horse-bells and the
noise of a crowd signal the arrival of the bridegroom.
As someone in the guest room say, "Oh, they're here,"
Relatives A,B,C, and D, Maeng Hyo-wŏn, and other
guests enter.)*

Relative A: We'll be meeting him sooner or later.

Relative B: Where's T'ae-ryang, the father-in-law-to-be?

Mr. Maeng: *(In a nagging tone)* Here, sir.

Kil-bo: *(Darts in.)* Sir, I can't find the bridegroom. He's missing, sir.

The Group: The bridegroom's missing?

Relative A: You must be out of your mind to say that. Who do you think is the one sitting on horseback over there? Don't you see the one in wedding clothes sitting proudly on the back of the horse over there?

Kil-bo: He's not the one coming here to get married, though. I tell you, the devil himself will be shocked. *(Exits in a hurry.)*

The Ch'ambong: (Darts in.) Oh dear, Mr. Maeng! Mr. Maeng!

Mr. Maeng: What's the matter with you all?

The Ch'ambong: He's not that. He's not that!

Mr. Maeng: Who's not what?

The Ch'ambong: I've got a world-shaking piece of news for you.

Mr. Maeng: Tell me, what do you mean by this?

The Ch'ambong: The eyes, shining bright as the morning star, are full of wisdom. The nose is brimming over with manly spirit. The arms and legs are full of vitality as they are powerfully built like iron hammers. The body is well-balanced and dignified like a man of virtue from heaven. All in all, the man has turned out to be completely different from the one we knew from rumor. What shall we do now?

Mr. Maeng: Be quiet. You've probably seen the wrong man. It's just impossible. Get out of my way. Seeing is believing. I'm going to take a look for myself. *(As he starts to exit, the goose-carrier enters at the head of a group of excited spectators accompanied by music. A considerable pause later the bridegroom enters. His face half veiled, looking royally handsome and strong-legged, Mi-ŏn is impressive as well as attractive. Everyone is simply dumbfounded and gives out cries of admiration. The womenfolk utter deep sighs of adoration. Mrs. Maeng steps out in front. An unexplained smile spreads around the lips of Kim Myŏng-jŏng who has come along as the groom's escort.)*

Mr. Maeng: Is that you? Are you the Mi-ŏn? *(Mi-ŏn intimates a soft "yes.")*

Mr. Maeng: Is it true that you are the son of P'ansŏ Kim?

Mi-ŏn: That is correct, sir. But why do you ask me that question? I wonder if this is not the residence of Chinsa Maeng. And I'm afraid I might have come to the wrong house. . . .

Mr. Maeng: (His heart starting to pound) No, you haven't. This is the right place. I'm Maeng T'ae-ryang. But my son-in-law. . . certainly my son-in-law is. . . come closer to me, young man.

(Mi-ŏn steps over to him as bidden.)

Mr. Maeng: (Growing utterly incredulous) No, that's not it. Keep walking a little more! Just a few more steps. Still that's not it. About face! Forward march! Ch'ambong, you certainly were right when you said you had a world-shaking piece of news for me!

The Ch'ambong: (Wiping his running nose) Just like I told you.

Mr. Maeng: Now, tell me, haven't you been a cripple?

Mi-ŏn: A cripple?

Mr. Maeng: My son-in-law's got to be a cripple. My son-in-law's supposed to be a lame one.

Kim Myŏng-jŏng: (Stepping forward) Sir!

Mr. Maeng: (With a start, a little later) I remember! It was you, wasn't it?

Kim Myŏng-jŏng: That's right, sir. I'll tell you a little about it. . . .

Mr. Maeng: Tell me about it? What about it?

Kim Myŏng-jŏng: I certainly told you so, and I am not denying it at all. But I talked it over with my cousin P'ansŏ Kim. . . .

Mr. Maeng: What? P'ansŏ Kim is your cousin?

Kim Myŏng-jŏng: Yes, sir. He's an elder cousin of mine.

Mr. Maeng: Then you were lying about being a wayfarer?

Kim Myŏng-jŏng: (Smiling) I trust you'll excuse me. As a matter of fact, I talked it over with my cousin before I made that up. And as for the reason. . . .

Mr. Maeng: What was the reason?

Kim Myŏng-jŏng: I can give it to you if you really want to know it. . . but rather than telling it to you myself, I think the bridegroom will speak to you about it at his own convenience in the future. I'm sorry to have caused so much trouble to you with such a fabrication. Therefore please accept my sincere apologies.

Mr. Maeng: What has made you. . . I mean what prompted you to make my family. . .? The Maeng family is going to be completely ruined!

Kim Myŏng-jŏng: Pardon me, sir? What do you mean by your family being ruined?

Mr. Maeng: Well! No, no, it's nothing. I just say things I don't really mean from time to time. It's a bad habit that I have—talking non, non, non, nonsense like that. So much for that now. We've got to get busy. Say, isn't there anybody there?

Kil-bo: Yes, sir.

Mr. Maeng: I want you boys to be on the alert so I won't have to yell each time I need you. Sneak out of here quickly and bring Kap-pun. . . .

Kil-bo: Sir, the Mistress Kap-pun is not here.

Mr. Maeng: Oh, you fool!

Hyo-wŏn: Ahem!

Mr. Maeng: (Looking at Hyo-wŏn and then Kim Myŏng-jŏng) Well, I just forgot to take care of the groom's escorts, Uncle. Ch'ambong, will you show the guests into the guest room?

The Ch'ambong: Yes, sir.

Hyo-wŏn: (To Kim Myŏng-jŏng) Sir, shall we go into the guest room?

(Kim Myŏng-jŏng and the escorts follow the Ch'ambong out to the guest room. The bridegroom steps over to the verandah. The crowd breaks up. Mr. Maeng, Mrs. Maeng, Hyo-wŏn, the Wet Nurse, Kil-bo, Relatives A,B,

C,D remain on stage to hold an emergency conference.)

Mr. Maeng: (In a tearful voice) Uncle, what shall we do?

Hyo-wŏn: What do you plan to do?

Mrs. Maeng: Let's send someone over to Ŭnsan-kol on horse-back, Uncle. How long will it take to get there by riding on the back of a mule?

Hyo-wŏn: On the back of a mule? Let me see. . . .

Relative A: Why use a mule, of all things?

Relative B: A donkey should be a bit faster.

Relative C: If you want something really fast, just use any horse after kicking it in the testicles.

Mr. Maeng: Say, darling!

Mrs. Maeng: Yes, dear. What is it?

Mr. Maeng: What is what? Wake up and see what's happening.

Mrs. Maeng: You don't need to make such a fuss. Nurse!

The Wet Nurse: Yes, Madam, I know what it is.

Mr. Maeng: Do whatever you can to delay the ceremony. In the meantime, Kil-bo, you hurry up and go get Kap-pun and bring her back here.

Kil-bo: I don't understand what you're up to. Don't you see that Kap-pun's being prettied up back there right in this house?

Mr. Maeng: (In a hushed tone) Listen, it's the real Kap-pun I mean.

Kil-bo: (In a hushed tone) Exactly, sir. That's just the way we made it up.

Mr. Maeng: You fool! *(In a whisper)* I don't mean Ip-pun, but I mean Kap-pun.

Kil-bo: (Also in a whisper) That's right, sir. You said you meant Kap-pun, not Ip-pun, didn't you? You really should be on the alert, sir.

Mr. Maeng: Oh, you knucklehead! Say, Sam-dol! *(Sam-dol rushes in.)*

Sam-dol: Yes, sir.

Mr. Maeng: I want you to run over and bring Kap-pun back

here right away. *(Sam-dol looks puzzled.)*

Kil-bo: (Still in a whisper, hysterically) I says, she's in the inner room.

Sam-dol: Bring Mistress Kap-pun, sir?

Mr. Maeng: Yes, and then I'll let you have Ip-pun right away. You've got to make the trip in an awful hurry, though.

Kil-bo: I see. You meant that other Mistress Kap-pun. *(Exits to the inner room.)*

Mr. Maeng: That's taken care of. Where there's a will, there's a way. So far, so good.

Relative B: If the bridegroom is here we ought to go ahead with the ceremony right away. It's improper to keep him waiting without giving him any good reason. I think you should bear this in mind and. . . .

Relative C: You're right. That's against *yangban* etiquette.

Mr. Maeng: Well, we just haven't had the time to take care of that etiquette problem, you see.

Kim Myŏng-jŏng: (Entering from the guest room) Sir, the bridegroom seems very tired from that long horseback trip. Would you please hold the ceremony as soon as possible?

Mr. Maeng: Certainly, sir. We'll hold it very soon.

Kim Myŏng-jŏng: Would you please make sure there's no delay?

Mr. Maeng: Delay's out of the question! We'll start it right away. . . except that the bride needs just a little more to finish up her make-up, sir.

Kim Myŏng-jŏng: Oh, no! The bride's not through with her make-up yet?

Mr. Maeng: Not exactly, sir. As a matter of fact, we've been waiting for the bride's grandfather to come and watch the ceremony, sir.

Kim Myŏng-jŏng: At any rate, I wish you would take your son-in-law's health into consideration and hold the ceremony right away. *(Exits.)*

Mr. Maeng: Say, Uncle, how far do you think Sam-dol has gone? Isn't it time yet for him to be heading back now?

Hyo-wŏn: Not even a winged horse could make it so soon. It might be different if he were wearing seven-league boots.

Mr. Maeng: Oh, heavens, what shall I do now?

Mrs. Maeng: Take it easy, dear. If there's no way out, we'll say the bride is sick.

Mr. Maeng: That's an idea. We could say the bride has gotten sick all of a sudden.

Mrs. Maeng: What do you think of it, all of you?

The Group: It's an excellent idea, too.

The Ch'ambong: (Entering from the guest room, in a hurry) Sir, the bride's grandfather's coming in.

Mr. Maeng: My father's coming in?

The Ch'ambong: He's in a towering rage, saying that this wedding shouldn't be allowed to take place, and he's so bitter. *(The Elder Maeng enters, trembling like the shadow of a skeleton, and stands upright.)*

The Elder Maeng: I hear you rascals are going to give my granddaughter away to a cripple—my only granddaughter and an only child in this family that we've brought up so tenderly. And you mean to do that by cheating me since I am hard of hearing and seeing? There must be some ulterior motives, you low-down rascals! Tell me the truth! Is it money? Or is it land? Tell me! *(The Group stands stock-still.)*

Mr. Maeng: Father, it's nothing of the sort, sir.

The Elder Maeng: You can't do that. No, you can't. Listen, T'ae-ryang, you fool! When I say "no" I mean it. Now show me that cripple. I want to take a look at my lame grandson-in-law. *(Stepping to the front of the verandah and taking a look, speaks haphazardly.)* Which one is it? Good heavens! What a brazen fellow you are! How dare a cripple like you try to marry someone in this family! You thick-skinned scapegrace!

Mr. Meang: Father! What you're saying is not true. Please take it easy and calm down.

The Elder Maeng: No, you can't do that. Take me up to the

verandah right away. I won't allow him in here even if it has to do with P'ansŏ Kim, nay, even if it has to do with the Prime Minister or somebody even higher. No, I won't.

Hyo-wŏn: That's not true any more, my dear elder brother. We thought so at first, too, but it's a different story now. Oh, no, you're going to hurt yourself if you try to get up there.

The Elder Maeng: Let me go! Get out of my way! I'm going to get up there without help. Get out of my way!

Hyo-wŏn: Oh, no, it's dangerous for you. *(The Elder Maeng tries to get on to the verandah, unyielding. Eventually Hyo-wŏn helps him onto the verandah.)*

The Elder Maeng: Hurry up and bring that rascal over to me! *(Kim Myŏng-jŏng shows up with Mi-ŏn at the gate.) (Taking a look around)* Humph, it's you! You're disgracing this respectable family of mine, because we've never allowed anyone in our family to marry a cripple from generation to generation. You may be an offspring of Sŭngji Kim, but that doesn't mean you can get away with what you're trying to do now. Get out of here, you rascal. Make yourself scarce before we throw you out!

(Mi-ŏn takes a few steps gently forward, making a deep bow with his hands in front.)

The Elder Maeng: Good Heavens! Just take a few more steps like that again, will you? *(Mi-ŏn turns around, takes a few more steps, and repeats the bowing.)* Oh dear, what does this mean? *(Surprised yet pleased)* Ha ha. After all, he's an off-spring of such a good family. Ha ha. T'ae-ryang! Why did you fool me about this boy being a cripple? From now on don't be so rash and thoughtless. Ho ho! I really shouldn't have taken those fellows' words seriously and gotten so excited about it. The bridegroom is an outstanding man. I didn't realize he's as intelligent-looking as a *Hwarang* boy, and as strong-legged as any man can be. Well, how is your father?

Mi-ŏn: Quite well, sir.

The Elder Maeng: What a handsome fellow you are. Your father should be proud of such a wonderful son. I wish you would forgive me for all the things I said without really knowing you. My granddaughter is a bit immature yet, but she's my precious grandchild and I want you to work together to make your marriage a happy one that lasts throughout the rest of your lives. Now, will you come on over to my side?

Mi-ŏn: Thank you, sir. *(Steps over and sits down beside the old man.)*

The Elder Maeng: T'ae-ryang!

Mr. Maeng: Yes, sir.

The Elder Maeng: How old am I now? Am I ninety or a few years over ninety? I've never been happier than now in all that time. First of all, my grandson-in-law's turned out to be a man of outstanding appearance. Second, you're a man of talent indeed, capable of choosing such a wonderful son-in-law. If these aren't things for me to rejoice at, what else is?

Mr. Maeng: Ahem! *(Smiles complacently.)*

The Elder Maeng: By the way, why didn't you start the ceremony yet?

Mr. Maeng: (Looking pale and worried) We'll get it started any time now, sir.

The Elder Maeng: I may die any day now. It could happen even today or tomorrow. So I want to see the happy event, the happy event of the Maeng family, get under way as soon as possible.

Mr. Maeng: Yes, sir. Right away, sir, if you'll just wait a few minutes, Father.

The Elder Maeng: What's keeping you from starting the last happy event of my life right away?

Mr. Maeng: Father! *(Asks his uncle to help him.)* Uncle!

The Elder Maeng: Listen, T'ae-ryang, you fool! Hyo-wŏn, you can. . . .

Mr. Maeng: Oh dear! *(Hurries over and whispers into his*

father's ear, only to turn away disappointed.) Ch'ambong!
Heavens, what shall I do? Go look out the entrance to the
village and see if she's on the way.

The Ch'ambong: Yes, sir. *(Rushes out.)*

The Elder Maeng: This is certainly not the way the *yangban*
does things. How could anyone keep the bridegroom
waiting so anxiously like this? Hurry up and get started!

Hyo-wŏn: We understand very well, my dear elder brother.
Please wait just a little while. Why should you be so im-
patient on a day like this?

The Elder Maeng: Oh, you unfilial bunch! What a way to talk
back! I'm an old man with my days numbered, and besides,
it's not going to cost you a lot of money to hold that
ceremony for me. . . Well, aren't you going to rush it up?

Mr. Maeng: Ch'ambong! *(Steps out. Hyo-wŏn, Mrs. Maeng,
and Relatives A and B hold a brief conference.)*

Kim Myŏng-jŏng: Well, what does this mean, sir?

Mr. Maeng: (Leaping to his feet) Pardon me, sir?

Kim Myŏng-jŏng: It's all very strange, sir. You still keep us
waiting. Has anything gone wrong again?

Mr. Maeng: No, sir. Nothing's gone wrong. The bride has
got a sudden pain in her chest—I mean she's got a toothache
and so. . . .

Kim Myŏng-jŏng: That's even more strange, sir. You said a
little while ago that you were waiting for the bride's
grandfather to attend the ceremony. . . .

Mr. Maeng: Yes, sir. A little while ago it was because of my
father. . . .

Kim Myŏng-jŏng: Are you really telling me the truth, sir?

Mr. Maeng: Yes, sir. I certainly am, sir.

Kim Myŏng-jŏng: Ha ha. I wonder if it isn't you yourself who
got sick—sick from waiting for that mule for so long.

Mr. Maeng: The mule?

Kim Myŏng-jŏng: Sir, a wedding ceremony is a solemn event
to begin with, and marriage a great human institution. If
you're not satisfied with the bridegroom in any way, we'll

just forget everything and go back home.

Mr. Maeng: No, not at all, sir. It's nothing of the sort, sir. *(Steps over to Ch'ambong, who enters disappointed.)* Ch'ambong!

The Ch'ambong: Yes, sir.

The Elder Maeng: Bring the bride out here. I'll hold the ceremony myself—the last happy event of my life. Oh, I see. You've been waiting for me to do so, eh! Why didn't you tell me so before? Well, Ch'ambong!

The Chambong: (*Hysterically*) Oh, what shall I do, sir?

Mr. Maeng: Uncle?

Hyo-wŏn: What could I do?

Mr. Maeng: Oh, God! Good God! Ch'ambong!

The Ch'ambong: (*Choked up*) Yes, sir. *(Exits to the inner room. Mrs. Maeng heaves a deep sigh. The Wet Nurse steps out to the verandah accompanied the Ch'ambong. Mi-ŏn stands facing her.)*

The Elder Maeng: Time flows like running water, for my adorable Kap-pun has already grown up big enough to get married. I may now be able to rest in peace, with you married to a good family. I'm so happy. I'm so delighted. I hadn't thought I'd be able to live long enough to attend this happy occasion. Ho ho.

(Kim Myŏng-jŏng smiles. Mr. Maeng, Mrs. Maeng, and Hyo-wŏn beat their breasts trying to contain themselves.)

— MUSIC —

Scene Two

The action takes place in the evening in the bridal chamber with its blind of beadwork pulled down. Mi-ŏn and Ip-pun are seated in front of the folding screen and there is a candle burning nearby. In front of the chamber Mr. Maeng, Kap-pun and the Ch'ambong are nervously waiting, all eager and anxious to see what's going to happen on the first night of the couple's wedding. In the dead calm of the evening, intermittently broken by the twittering of birds and the chirping of insects, Ip-pun is squatting down in the candlelight which is dancing like the shimmering air.

Mi-on: Kap-pun! Kap-pun! *(Tries to hold her by the wrist.)* *(Ip-pun draws back in surprise.)*

Mi-ŏn: What's the matter with you? Why have you been dodging me all this time? *(Pause)* Is it because you don't like me? *(Pause)* I suppose that's what it is. You certainly don't like me, do you?

   (Ip-pun is awe-struck, not knowing what to do with herself.)

Mi-ŏn: Kap-pun! We're now man and wife who swore by the gods of heaven and earth at the ceremony that we would love each other and stick together the rest of our lives. But that arrangement was a mere formality. What is more important than that is our mind and love for each other. If you don't like me, however, please say so, Kap-pun.

Ip-pun: No, not at all, sir. It's nothing of the sort, sir.

Mi-ŏn: (Smiling) Well? What could it be, then?

   (Ip-pun cringes again.)

Mi-ŏn: That's right! I know what it is. You're a bit too tired from that ceremony this afternoon. Isn't that what it is? If so, I should have let you go to sleep in good time! Well, let's go to bed. *(Tries to put out the candle.)*

Ip-pun: (Stopping him from putting out the candle.) Please don't! Please don't, sir!

Mi-ŏñ: Please don't? Please don't what? *(Caresses Ip-pun's shoulder tenderly.)· (Ip-pun, unable to control her tears, tries to run away, rolling up the bead-string blind.)*

Mi-ŏn: (Holding her affectionately) Darling! What's the matter with you?

Ip-pun: Nothing, sir. Let me go now. If you really insist, you'll be disgracing yourself and making a serious blunder. Don't let that happen to you, sir.

Mi-ŏn: Disgrace myself? Make a serious blunder?

Ip-pun: Yes, sir. I'm not Kap-pun.

Mi-ŏn: Don't say that. You're my wife Kap-pun!

Ip-pun: Oh my, what shall I do? You don't seem to know anything about it yet. I'm just a poor maidservant. I. . . I've been tending my mistress Kap-pun. . . I'm scared. Scared of Heaven. But I had no choice but to follow my master's direction and take the place of Kap-pun. I knew how wrong it was, but he kept after me to do so and I had to oblige, sir.

Mi-ŏn: (Smiling) Is that right?

Ip-pun: (Starts crying.) I hope you would forgive me, sir. To tell you the truth, my mistress Kap-pun said she'd rather die than marry you, because she thought you were a cripple. That's why a poor maidservant like me had to be brought in as a substitute bride to meet the bridegroom who was already on his way here. So I'm just a fraud.

Mi-ŏn: Well. . . .

Ip-pun: And I thought you were a cripple, too, sir. I thought it was the case of a lonely *yangban* who couldn't marry any girl or get any girl to marry him. Now, I'm surprised to see that you're not a cripple. But I do wish you were one, a lonely cripple that no other girl would pay any attention to. I don't like you being so different from what I had expected, sir. I wish you would forgive me—one of the wicked people who cheated you. *(Cries.)*

Mi-ŏn: Listen, darling, the one who really should apologize and ask for forgiveness is me.

Ip-pun: Pardon me, sir?

Mi-ŏn: Because I knew it all along. You didn't think I knew what was going on, did you?

Ip-pun: No, I didn't, sir. . . .

Mi-ŏn: (Holding Ip-pun tenderly by the wrist) Don't be surprised now. It's I who set this all up. I'm the one who did it. I was the one who asked Uncle Myŏng-jŏng to spread the rumor that I was a cripple.

Ip-pun: Really, sir?

Mi-ŏn: Only I didn't know it would end up troubling you like this.

Ip-pun: Sir, what made you do such. . . .

Mi-ŏn: What made me do that? Can't you figure it out? Couldn't you guess why I played such a trick, and what made me set this all up?

Ip-pun: I don't think I could, sir.

Mi-ŏn: I wanted to find out the weight and depth of a human mind, especially a woman's mind. Whether one is a cripple, a beggar, a rich man, or a poor one has to do with superficial things. I've known enough of rich and prosperous people to get sick and tired of their shallow minds. The kind of mind I'm looking for is a genuine one like yours. I learned through my uncle that you have a mind firm and honest enough to overcome any kind of problems, troubles or worries. You're the very type of wife I've been looking for. I now feel immensely happy as if I were touching a genuine mind.

Ip-pun: Sir! But I'm still a. . . ..

Mi-ŏn: Don't mention it now. You're neither a maidservant nor a mistress, but my wife. I'm simply overjoyed at the strength and beauty of your genuine mind and true love. What gives a man real pleasure in life is to be able to get hold of something that is lofty, fragrant, and precious. Do you understand?

Ip-pun: Yes, sir. *(Goes into his arms. Each looks at the other.)*

Mi-ŏn: Now, stop sirring me, Ip-pun.

Ip-pun: Yes. . . .

Mi-ŏn: I'm nobody to be sirred by you. I'm just your husband. Now try calling me what I am to you.

Ip-pun: How shall I call you?

Mi-ŏn: Isn't there a word wives use to call their husbands? What do they call them?

Ip-pun: I don't know.

Mi-ŏn: What's the word they usually say when they call their husbands? Isn't it "dear" or "darling"? Now, go ahead and try it on me.

Ip-pun: I don't know. . . .

Mi-ŏn: Come on, come on.

Ip-pun: (In a tiny voice) Well. . . heavens, I don't know.

Mi-ŏn: Come on! Hurry up and say it!

Ip-pun: Darling, sir!

Mi-ŏn: No, not that.

Ip-pun: Sir, darling!

Mi-ŏn: No, not that either.

Ip-pun: Say, darling! *(Buries her face in her skirt before quite finishing the phrase.)*

(Mi-ŏn holds Ip-pun in his arms. Starts to undo her trinkets and bridal dress, take off his own clothes; puts out the candle.)

Kap-pun: Mother, the candle's been put out.

Mrs. Maeng: Oh, my goodness, what can I do now? It's all your father's fault. It's because you've got such a smart father.

Kap-pun: Mother! *(Exits to the front. Mrs. Maeng follows her out and runs into Mr. Maeng.)*

Mrs. Maeng: (Glaring at him) Going to the dogs! I say we're going to the dogs!

Kap-pun: You fool, Father! Drop dead! *(Exits. Pause. The Ballad of Toraji sung by an unknown singer is heard.)* *(Mr. Maeng collapses on the floor after standing distraught for some time.)*

Sam-dol: Aren't you going to make good your promise to me, my dear father-in-law?

Mr. Maeng: Good Lord! What shall I do with this fellow?

CURTAIN

The Fourth Class Car*

by Ch'a Pŏm-sŏk
translated by Edward D. Rockstein

Characters

Old Man
His Daughter-in-law
Merchant

Woman
Conductor
Four or five passengers

Place

The platform between the sleeping car and the third class car of the night train to Seoul.

---

* The Fourth Class Car: There were only *1st, 2nd,* and *3rd* class on Korean trains at this time. The *1st* class was for U.N. personnel only. The *2nd* class was reserved seats for those who could afford them. The *3rd* class was usually stuffed with riders struggling for seats and/or standing room.

Time

The present. End of the past year. (Note: 1956 would be the approximate year, based on publication date of the play.)

Stage

The passage and boarding platform connecting the sleeping and third class cars. On the right, the door to the third class car is open about half-way and passengers who haven't been able to find seats are being pushed out. On the left, a door with "SLEEPING CAR" painted on its thick glass window is shut tightly. Two or three of the sleeping car windows covered with grass-green curtains are visible. In the background deserted, cold winter fields flow on by like a river. Here and there a patch of white snow is seen. On the passageway, passengers and baggage are crammed closely together. Everything is so crowded that one can just barely pass. However, in front of the sleeping car door there are several spaces and one gets the feeling that it is an "Off Limits—Entry Forbidden" area. The passengers are all hunkering or sitting. The time is winter, a few days before the New Year. It is the time of day when evening is turning into night.

When the curtain rises, the sounds of men shouting and the cries of women yelling something or other begin to be heard from within the third class car. However, on the passageway there is only the sense of depressed fatigue and the monotonous sound of the wheels.

Man's voice: Push me, eh? Look old lady. . . .
Woman's voice: Hey. . . you're crushing my baby. . . .
Man's voice: Ah, pipe down. . . if you don't like it here.
(Sounds of coarse laughter. After a little while the con-

ductor *is barely able to elbow his way through the crowd
and emerges from the third class car.)*

Conductor: Tickets, please. *(He looks at each person's ticket.
The passengers sit silently like robots thrusting their tickets
out mechanically in turn.)*

A: (Holding out his ticket) About when do we get to Seoul?

Conductor: (Extremely businesslike) Around twenty-two
hundred.

A: Uuh? You say twenty-two hundred?

Conductor: (Crossing over to the next person) That means
ten o'clock.

A: But the schedule said seven. . . .

Conductor: The train is scheduled to be delayed about three
hours.

B: Oh, so now they even have *scheduled* delays these days?

Conductor: Well, what do you want me to. . . . *(He is just
about to pass on, when suddenly he notices a large suitcase.)* Uh-oh, who stuck their bag here? Who's the owner?
No one? *(He kicks it a couple of times.)*

Merchant: (Looking up) Please don't kick it, they'll break.

Conductor: If you leave your bag in the way, what am I
supposed to do? Wouldn't it have been better to check it?

Merchant: I'm sorry.

Conductor: Would someone who knows what "sorry" means
have done this?

Merchant: I couldn't just check it because of the eggs.

Conductor: Eggs you say? But that's your problem, you have
to think about the comfort of the passengers!

Merchant: (As he pulls the bag aside.) I'm sorry. From now
on. . . .

Conductor: Eh. Well! *(Crosses over to the sleeping car. In
front of the door he shakes a woman lying there nursing a
child.)*
Hey! Lady!

Woman: (In a feeble voice) But there's no room, how. . .?

Conductor: No room, why no room. . . if you stay here and

roll off, how would that be? (*Without answering the woman shifts obliquely. She is like a soulless wraith because of her hunger and exhaustion. Conductor puffs and chokes on his breath. Steps inside the door. Everyone lapses into silence for a while. The train's whistle emits a long sob and passes on.*)

Merchant: (Grumbling to himself) Think of the passengers. . . shh! Well, does he think that I'm not a passenger? I paid my thousand *hwan** too! I bought my ticket, but I'm not a passenger?

(*At this moment an old man and his daughter-in-law, who is dripping with sweat, practically fall out of the third class car. The old man is in a worn-out cotton overcoat. He constantly wears his old felt hat which is chestnut color in name only. It is evident from his daughter-in-law's appearance that she still has a touch of the young girl in her. . . she is wrapped up to her nose in a shawl woven of cotton yarn. Her stomach readily announces that she is in the middle of a pregnancy. She holds a large wicker basket in her hand.*)

Old Man: Eht. Just twice through that bastard's car and I've ripped the crotch of my pants. (*As he smoothes the wrinkled crease of his pants, he searches for a place to sit down.*) Is this place full, too?

Daughter-in-law: (Indicating the front of the sleeping car) Father, there's an empty place over there. . . .

Old Man: So, let's get over there. Careful, my trousers are bound to get snagged. (*The two carefully cross the passageway like blind men and sit beside the woman.*)

Old Man: (Pulls the overcoat up around his chin and sits.) If I'd known there was a space like this. . . went through all that trouble in that living hell for nothing. . . you sit down, too!

Daughter-in-law: (Sits carefully.) Father, you'll ruin your

---

* *hwan:* Unit of currency.

coat, here spread this. . . . *(She starts to unwind her scarf.)*

Old Man: That's alright. It's cold; we'll put it around us both.

Daughter-in-law: I'm dying from the heat. . . .*(Lets out a sigh.)*

Old Man: The wind's cold, but isn't this better than all that shoving in there?

Daughter-in-law: Yuh! I nearly died getting out of there. It's a little better now.

Old Man: (Blows his nose and then as he strokes his beard.) Dammit! To have to pay money to go through this. . . .

Merchant: (Pulls a pint of whiskey out, puts it to lips and drinks.) Tomorrow's *Training Day* and there'll probably be a lot of people. . . .

Old Man: Unfortunately, that's true. *(Slips a cigarette out of his pack and says to his daughter-in-law.)* I don't know if we can find Pok-t'ae without a hassle.

Daughter-in-law: (Pulls an envelope out from her bosom.) If we just go by this, how can we find him. . .?

Old Man: (Smoking cigarette) Say, is that bastard alive there? *(Indicating the wicker basket beside his daughter-in-law)*

Daughter-in-law: (Looks into the basket. A chicken, sticks of cooking charcoal, a pot, etc., can be seen sticking out.)

Old Man: (Laughs satisfiedly.) So he's still alive, eh? *(Silence)* Weren't we going to bring one more?

Daughter-in-law: (Laughing sweetly) Even you, Father, no matter how much chicken you say you can eat, how can you put two chickens in one mouth? . . . Shall we spend the hours visiting while he's cooking?

Old Man: Two or three chickens at a sitting just to melt the frost in the morning; what's more, they say that training makes one very hungry. *(Daughter-in-law turns her head and rubs her eyes a couple of time.)*

Merchant: (Glancing over sideways) Are you going to see your son?

Old Man: Huh? Yes. . . .

Merchant: The transition is rough for an old man.

Old Man: Me, I'm alright, but the children. . . . *(Looks at his daughter-in-law.)*

Merchant: Have a nice visit. When you're at the training center, the best thing is when the folks from home come for a visit.

Old Man: Even though we tried to go once before, this little cat has to scratch out a living all day on a few acres of land in order to live, and that's about the size of it. She's been planning to come out since the autumn harvest. Now it's really become a big occasion. She's worked herself to be able even to come out like this with one hand empty. To country folks like us it seems like we're being shoved about helter-skelter and trampled. *(Finally the merchant drinks the whiskey and wipes off the mouth of the bottle.)*

Merchant: Nowadays this thing called life gobbles us up like that. Even though we spend money earned with tears of blood to buy a ticket, when we try to find a seat, we have to go through a living war. . . . The price is outrageous and while I sit here on the floor like this, I'm ordered to sit sideways. When I was looking for a spot *(He indicated the Old man's place with his chin.)* to sit down, I was chased away, "This is the Sleeping Car." It feels like we are rats trapped in a jar being teased. *(Gradually becoming drunk)* If you close your eyes and make one false step, it's the end of everything! *(Looks down at the road bed.)*

Old Man: We have to live. Just being happy is the heart of the matter.

Merchant: Old Man, you still have hope—because you have a live son and you also have a charming daughter-in-law. But it's my lot to have just one unmarried daughter by my old wife. Dammit to hell! If I had only just one son, the strength to live would spurt out of me as never before. That's my wish.

Old Man: You make your living as a merchant, don't you?

Merchant: Living? Humph, what kind of world do you think

this is now, that people like us could make a living without suffering? Does it seem that I'm waiting for money? Because I go on living without starving, it's a living, but. . . .

Old Man: Everything's alright if you don't starve.

Merchant: (Voice rising) Is something to eat so much? When I first became involved in peddling, I would sleep huddled up in a flophouse in front of Seoul Station and then ride back on the train.

Old Man: Don't you live in Seoul? I've heard that the people there are not like us in the southern provinces. . . .

Merchant: My home is in North Korea. I escaped South during the war, but I've been robbed of sons and brothers to give me a hand and I had to enter a refugee camp for a while because I had neither relatives to support me nor home to stay in. And so I began peddling eggs to keep my wife and daughter from starving. Even that these days. . . we haven't put aside any of the New Year's eggs to hatch chicks. Just getting these *(Indicating the suitcase full of eggs with his chin)* took three days. *(Sighs.)* The older I get, the tougher life gets. It seems as though the whole world has abandoned me and I just run about aimlessly like this train.

Old Man: Nonetheless, life has to be lived. I'm only an ignorant man who has gone on just living and farming for sixty years in a corner of a little village, but this past summer when our Pok-t'ae was drafted, the cold cut me to the bone and I lost the will to live. Yet, it wasn't long thereafter that *(Looks around to his daughter-in-law who sits there quietly staring at the scenery flowing by.)* I could see that a grandson was coming. My spirits were lifted and even though there was this bone-chilling cold, I only had thoughts of living. What are children? Huh ho. . . . *(Laughs to himself.)*

Merchant: When you're raising kids the strength to live comes. What's the use of earning money, having a position, or doing something in a world like this? It's a world of thieves!

Old Man: Even so, that fools like us, you and me, have to earn money without anything really to do burns me up.

Merchant: Just so; thieves! However loud I complain, complain that it is all set up so neatly, is it really so that the peasant can live well? Parents love a child and they give him government to live by, but bastards like us have to go on like this. Everything they say they are doing for us is a pack of lies. Just take a look into that car! Well, this so-called world is all like this. . . .

Old Man: Really, it's so. . . .

Merchant: Even so, because I even lie in order to eat and live, the world is comfortable, hahhah. *(Pause)* If my children had lived, it would have been so much better. . . .

Old Man: Didn't you say you had a daughter. . . .

Merchant: Marry off a daughter and what do you do? It must be a son!

Old Man: Haha. . . still there are old men trying to live on their children's generosity. *(The daughter-in-law pulls the basket to her and takes out three or four pieces of kimbab*.)*

Daughter-in-law: Father, have some. . . .

Old Man: (Takes one and holds it out.) You eat one, too. Go ahead. *(Hands one to the merchant.)*

Merchant: Ah, no thank you. I just had some whiskey and I have no taste for food now. Please, go ahead. *(Pulls out his money from his pocket and counts it. The woman with the baby looks across at him furtively.)*

Old Man: Well. . . however, it's not right for just us to eat. . . . *(He looks all around. At this time the woman who awhile earlier sat down behind him looks over hungrily at the food and their glances meet.)*

Old Man: Won't you take one of these?

Woman: (Lights up with joy but holds back at the same time.) O.K. . . . you go ahead and eat and I'll take what's

---

* *kimbab:* Rice and vegetables rolled in seaweed.

left. . . .

Daughter-in-law: Have one, a baby's mother has to eat for two so she can have her milk. . . .

Woman: Well, just one. . . . *(Accepts one and begins to devour it.)*

Daughter-in-law: (Also eating hers) You're really hungry. . . .

Woman: To tell the truth, I haven't eaten since breakfast. . . .

Old Man: So it's like that, eh. . . well, why didn't you say so then, and. . . .

Merchant: Doesn't she look like that's so? I was wondering where she was going so hungry in this cold winter. . . . *(Stares across at her.)* How far are you going?

Woman: (Stops eating and begins crying, sobbing deeply.)

Daughter-in-law: Now, now, why're you crying? Hunh?

Old Man: You're not ill, are you?

Woman: (Clutches the sleeping child tightly against her breasts and continues to sob heavily. The other three, not knowing her reason, can only look at each other.)

Merchant: (To the old man) It seems as though she's probably had some misfortune, doesn't it?

Old Man: I'd say so.

Daughter-in-law: Why are you crying like this?

Woman: (Wipes away her tears and takes a couple of deep breaths.) I'm mad! I'm a slut who should be killed. *(Pause)* Thank you. Thank you. It's really been a long while since I've been treated with such warmth and kindness, but enough. . . .

Old Man: It's alright. At first glance it probably seems to you that there is reason to feel like this but. . . has there ever been a time in this world when things always turned out the way one wished? One can just live out the days of his life. . . and rightly so because there's another world yet. . . .

Woman: But there is no bitch so unfortunate as me; it would have been better in this case of this lump of blood had never been born. In a tough world like this my child is no better than my enemy.

Old Man: What! What kind of talk is this? Calling children enemies. . . cursing and screaming recklessly like this will bring down Heaven's punishment upon you.

Woman: (In a desperate tone) You say that this perverse God has punishments to give me? I figure I've lived the whole thirty years of my life just receiving Heaven's punishments! *(Again her tears flow.)*

Merchant: Oh ho. . . I'd been thinking that I was the most unfortunate being in the world, but it appears that here is someone even more unfortunate than me.

Woman: Even more than unfortunate, so put upon that I can't go on living. If I can lessen this load even one day sooner, I want to do it. And since there are many orphanages in Seoul, I am on my way there to turn over my baby.

Merchant: (Greatly surprised) This baby?

Woman: It's no deep mystery. If I go around with this on my back, I won't even be able to feed myself. If I have this baby, even though I stop to being a kitchen maid, who could use me?

Old Man: Well, is this your only child?

Woman: I have a daughter; my mother's mother is lending a hand with her and she's been left with her for the time being.

Merchant: If that's so, couldn't you leave this one with her, too?

Woman: She's my mother's family but I can't be too much in her debt. When a grandchild is doing well, they are charming, but if you show up at the gate like this with no husband, no money, and no house, rather than charm, there's fire in their eyes.

Old Man: This is terrible. You're saying that this world has reached the point where the moral relationship between parent and child* has broken down completely!

Woman: When the baby's father was alive, we were living

---

* Refers to one of the five relationships in the Confucian system.

the comfortable life of wage-earners, but last year he was killed in an auto accident as he was leaving work and so now even the attitude of my parents, brothers, and sisters has changed.

Merchant: Well, what have you decided to do when you get to Seoul?

Woman: Will I be ashamed to choose between good and bad in feeding my family? As time goes on, I'll have to do something to earn money. And so I will be able to call my daughter who's staying with my grandmother back to me.

Old Man: Perhaps so. Since it's the rule that children who eat their parent's gruel and rice should care for their parents.

Merchant: (Sinks into thought.) Is this child also a girl?

Woman: No, sir. It's a boy. Well, men say that boys are better and everyone is happy to have a boy, but I never dreamed that I really would have to starve like this. If there was someone who wanted a child, I'd rather give it to him right now.

Daughter-in-law: My G. . . .

Merchant: (Excited) Is that really so?

Woman: What's all the fuss, do you think I'm sitting here fooling you? It's because I think that to do this is one kind of love which I as his mother can give him. In fact, several times before I've had it in mind to jump into the river with him on my back, but there seems to be something about dying without a chance. I felt it would be better not to d. . . . *(Cries again.)*

Old Man: But, if you give this child away to someone, how could you live?

Woman: I'm giving him up in order to live. Since he's a child I want to be rid of, someone who wants a child should have him. If I hand him over to such a person, it would be better than his living in an orphanage. . . . Since his mother can't feed herself, it is an empty joke for him to suck on my teat like this. *(Baby cries.)*

Daughter-in-law: (Looking at him with sympathy) Now. . . now. . . don't cry! I'll give you one of these. *(Takes a dried persimmon from her basket and offers it to him, but the child just cries harder.)*

Woman: (With a face full of tears) Cry! Cry! My teats are dry! What do you want from me! You enemy. . . . *(She hits him on the backside. The background earlier was an enveloping darkness, now the train is passing through village after village with lights flickering like shooting stars. Occasionally the screaming train whistle sounds plaintively.)*

Merchant: (Has been deep in thought for a while but now takes his money from his pocket and counts it.)

Woman: (Wipes her eyes.) Eh?

Merchant: Would you give him to me?

Woman: (With a half-believing, half-suspicious expression) Eh?

Merchant: Since bastards like me have become so bold, perhaps you feel that you can't believe me, but if you give him to me, there is no doubt that I would raise him as my true son.

Woman: But how would your wife feel about. . .?

Merchant: She always goes along with me. We had a couple of sons, too, but they were taken away by those Communist sons of bitches while we were in the North. . . now we have just a ten-year-old girl and we are always saying how wonderful it would be if we only had a son. They say that if you have money everything will be alright, but how can we just live for money?

Old Man: That's so. Money and power are things men live for, but since children come from God. . . .

Merchant: I can tell from what you've said that your circumstances are bad and that you seem to be destitute. If you give me the baby, in the future you will be freer to pursue your own affairs. Since I will be as happy as I can be, won't it be the best for everyone? Yunh? How about it?

Woman: But. . . .

Merchant: But what? You don't like what I'm suggesting?

Woman: Is there any reason not to like it? It's because the very thing I was wishing for before suddenly, unexpectedly happened. . . somehow my soul feels empty and I feel like all my strength has suddenly evaporated! *(Looks down on the baby pityingly.)*

Old Man: So it is. . . of course it's so! Why wouldn't it break your heart to get rid of the child you've sliced up your life to share with, whether you're well-off or not?

Merchant: I understand. But when I talk like this I don't know what you will think, but because this will show my good faith, here, please accept this. *(Pulls out the wad of bills.)* It's 10,000 *hwan*. It's my business capital, but since what you need on the spot is money, please accept this .

Woman: (Intends to accept the money without saying a word, looks at the baby and starts sobbing heavily. The baby is startled and also begins to cry.)

Merchant: Well, take this and give me the baby. What's the use of going on crying like this? *(The woman brushes away the tears and gives him the baby. The merchant accepts the baby, hugs him, and wraps him up. The woman, devastated, takes the money and puts it in her bosom.)*

Merchant: Oh ho,. . . this little beggar's eyes are really cute! So large. . . who's he take after?

Old Man: Take after, who do you think he takes after?

Merchant: Yunh? Well, I guess he resembles me! Ha, ha! *(Looks at the baby.)* Is that so? Uuh. A boy has to look like his father! *(For some reason the baby stops crying.)*

Merchant: It seems this rascal understands. He's smiling, laughing, . . . that's right. . . that's right. . . Hum, Hum. . . *(To the woman)* by the way, I have to know his name, month and hour of birth so. . . .

Woman: We called him 'T'ae-jin.' He was born on the twenty-third of the month of the winter solstice (11th lunar month). . . on his 100th day anniversary which just passed I offered rice cakes but I can't even get a plate of vegetables. . . . *(Cries again.)*

Merchant: (Staring at the baby) Now when we go home, let's have a new anniversary party. . . that's right. . . just so. . . shall I buy you a pair of pants? No? Well, a colored night-shirt? Good? Ha, ha.

Old Man: Really, isn't this fate? This little brat who cried so much playing like this?

Daughter-in-law: (Giving him the dried persimmon she'd taken out earlier) Eat this. That's good. . . take it and eat it. It really is fate.

Woman: Thank you. The world seems to be opening up for me. That the thing I tortured myself over for I don't know how long can be accomplished so easily like this. . . . It looks like I've got to believe that God might even help a person once in a while.

Merchant: I think so, too. Starting tomorrow, even though I break both my arms, I'll earn my living. . . . I'll have to raise this rascal so he'll never have to envy a soul. Even if it be my dead children! Old man, now I, too, have a son! Before I had no son, but suddenly a handsome son like this has appeared. Ha, ha! *(As though the train itself were in better spirits it gives a long blast with its whistle and rushes on.)*

Old Man: What did I tell you? Didn't I say that you have to try to live out your life? Ho, ho!

Woman: Well, please raise him well by all means. When he grows up to be a fine person don't forget this unfortunate woman. . . .

Merchant: I understand. You gave birth to this baby but as the raising is up to me. . . no matter what, he will grow up to be a fine person, set your mind at ease.

Woman: Well, I'll be getting off at the next stop. I have some stuff and I have to go in there to get it. I'll be back in a minute.

Merchant: Take care.

Old Man: Please, take good care of yourself if I don't see you again.

Woman: Yes. . . it's been nice meeting you, too, young lady. *(Woman exits into the 3rd class car to the right. The merchant hugs the baby. The old man stares after her.)*

Merchant: He's really handsome. He's thin because he hasn't been able to eat enough, but his bones are strong. Our eldest looked like this before. . . come. . . come. . . .

Old Man: Are you so happy?

Merchant: (Looking around) Yuh? Yes. . . I just want to hold him like this all night.

Daughter-in-law: (To herself) Somehow I just can't believe it. Can such things be?

Old Man: What?

Daughter-in-law: I somehow can't help being suspicious of her.

Old Man: What do you suspect?

Daughter-in-law: Well, no matter how poor her life may be, would she be able to give her child away to someone like this? A child carved out of her own flesh and blood over ten months. . .?

Old Man: On the contrary if you were starving, couldn't you?

Daughter-in-law: Even so. . . .

Old Man: Right now you don't have anything special to worry about. Could you take someone else's child?

Daughter-in-law: Who knows? These days the world is so foul. . . .

Merchant: What are you talking about?

Old Man: Well, my daughter-in-law was wondering whether she could believe the woman.

Merchant: You think that this isn't her child?

Daughter-in-law: Well, she said. . . earlier when she took the money it seemed like some kind of business. . . where do they have mothers who take money while handing their children over the strangers? They're not goods. . . .

Merchant: When you're really hungry, doesn't even muddy water look like gruel?

Daughter-in-law: However poor she says she may be, though, it's suspicious that she doesn't even want to know your address. Really, if that's like a mother. . . where can you find a mother who will tell you something like wanting raise her child in some stranger's home and then, well, take 10,000 *hwan* and just turn over her child?

Old Man: Ummm. . .

Merchant: However this came about, there is no doubt that from today on this is my son! Whoever says anything about. . . it's alright to lose 10,000 *hwan* if a boy like this from somewhere. . . 'T'ae-jin'. . . . That's right! *(The baby starts to cry again.)*

Merchant: It seems as though he's starving. . . . *(Looks around.)* It'd be best if I got him some milk. . . .

Old Man: Where could you get milk?

Merchant: They should have it at the station, but it may be so crowded that I can't get off.

Old Man: Please go while the train is stopped.

Merchant: Yes, there is nothing else to do! Ah. . . don't cry! Dooh. . . dooh. . . the next time the train stops, I'll buy you some milk. . . . *(The train whistle blows two long blasts and the train's speed seems to be slackening as it draws near the next stop.)*

Merchant: (To the daughter-in-law) Excuse me, Miss, but would you look after him for a little while, please? I want to run and get some milk for. . . .

Daughter-in-law: Yes. *(Takes the child, hugs, and soothes him, but the child cries all the harder. As the train is about to stop, the stationmaster passes with a lantern in his hand calling out the name of the station. The noise of passengers getting on and off increase gradually.)*

Merchant: Well, for just a minute. . . . *(Jumps down toward backstage.)*

Old Man: The people of this world will all knock themselves out for the sake of a child, somehow, I don't know how they fight on to live. . . *(Two or three of the passengers who had been sitting behind him also get off. At this time, the woman comes by on the station platform and makes as if to get back on again.)*

Woman: Young lady!

Daughter-in-law: Yes! *(Looks around.)*

Woman: Give the child here.

Daughter-in-law: The child?

Woman: *(Extremely impatiently)* Over there a minute ago that gentleman asked me to come and breast-feed the child quickly before the train pulls out. I'll feed him in there beside the fire and then be off.

Daughter-in-law: But where did he. . .?

Woman: *(Angrily)* Quick give him to me! The train will leave soon. He's calling from over there!

Old Man: Go ahead. The most costly medicine in the world is nothing next to mother's milk. *(Daughter-in-law hands over the baby but maintains a suspicious expression.)*

Woman: *(With a sobbing voice)* My dear, T'ae-jin! Won't you have a little of mommy's teat? So. . . . *(Pinches his cheek.)* Well, I'll feed you and turn you over to your father.

　　(Disappears into the darkness.)

Old Man: It seems difficult to break off the relationship between mother and child after all. However bad things were, could I hand my child over to someone?

Daughter-in-law: I truly don't know if I could. If she could get married again, it wouldn't have to be so. . . . *(At this time the bell rings signalling that the train is about to pull out.)*

Daughter-in-law: What's happening? The train's leaving, but. . .?

Old Man: Careful, don't fall off! *(Then the merchant, carrying a bottle of milk jumps up as the train begins to move.)*

Merchant: Eht! I ran all along the whole station trying to find this bottle of milk and. . . .

Daughter-in-law: But didn't you bring the baby back with you?

Merchant: Yunh? Baby?

Old Man: Why did you leave the baby and come back?

Merchant: Leave the baby and return? I asked the young lady to look after the child, and. . . .

Daughter-in-law: Oh, oh, didn't you have the baby's mother come back. . . .?

Merchant: What do you mean? I ran all around looking for milk but. . . .

Daughter-in-law: Something's wrong, something's. . . . *(Acts very nervously.)*

Merchant: She took him away?

Daughter-in-law: Yes, she said that you had asked her to feed the baby and then. . . .

Old Man: It's not clear, the train was about to go and everything happened so fast. . . .

Merchant: (Sits heavily.) Something terrible nearly happened! *(Sighs.)*

Old Man: Hunh? *(Merchant suddenly laughs out loud.)*

Merchant: She tried to fool me with an out-and-out lie to steal my hard earned money! But she didn't fool me! Ha, ha!

Merchant: Of course it wasn't 10,000. It was a few 10 *hwan* bills wrapped around a wad of paper. I switched it in my pocket, didn't it look suspicious?

Old Man: (Uncomprehending) Can it be that. . .?

Merchant: Old Man, today the world is such a place. God only knows who can straighten it out and make it better. Now she can't even stop at an inn for fear of seeing me! Ha, ha. *(Old man and daughter-in-law sit with mouths open as train turns on into the darkness.)*

Merchant: (Laughs.) Well, I'll drink this warm milk. *(Drunks as the curtain falls.)*

A New Common Sense

by Yi Kŭn-sam
translated by Yi T'ae-dong
and Greggar Sletteland

Characters

Kim Sang-bŏm
Kim Sang-hak, a rocket expert, his elder brother
Kim Sang-ch'ŏl, his younger brother
President, of a Steel Company
Sŏng A-mi, Secretary, President's daughter-in-law
Tank, lover of Hyŏn So-hi
Hyŏn So-hi, mistress of Tank
Manager, of the apartment building in which Kim Sang-bŏm lives
Pak Yong-ja, a girl who lives in the apartment
Mrs. Mun, Pak Yong-ja's mother
Pae Yŏng-min, Business Manager

Stage

The stage can represent an apartment, the office of a company, and streets in various ways. But it should not necessarily be realistic. In general, the right side of the stage is the interior of the apartment; the left side, the office of a company. The front downstage area is used as corridors, streets and a park. Though the space between the audience and the interior of the apartment is vacant, it is imagined that there is a wall standing there. The stage in front of the interior is also used as the corridor of the apartment. When, outside of the present situation, the characters in this play reminisce or recall their memories, they can have freedom of space.

A deep-voiced church bell tolls. The curtain rises. Before us is the interior of an apartment. As the bell rings, Kim Sang-bŏm gets out of bed, giving a yawn; he has just slipped on his trousers with his upper-pajamas over his shoulder. Rubbing his eyes with one hand, he pulls the window curtains apart. The golden sunshine of a clear morning floods into his room. After he stretches himself to the limit, he does a few indoor calisthenics. His shoulders throb with a deep pain and he has a backache. At the age of 31 he seems visited by these phenomena too early. Then he gathers various magazines which are scattered on the sofa and the floor. He comes front stage and turns to the audience.

Sang-bŏm: This Sunday morning I feel very tired, because I couldn't get to sleep all night long. But I don't have any particular anxiety about my insomnia, nor did I drink too much either, the way a healthy wage-earner usually would on a Saturday night. It's just because of these damn magazines. I'm talking about these American magazines, for one of which I paid two hundred *wŏn* in the alley behind the Ch'ŏnil Bank. Of course, I can't read them, because they are written in English. I'm a college graduate, but I have no interest in English. I don't think I lack a talent for language. I would rather believe that the poor teaching methods of the current college English teachers made me miserable like this. At least, I must have some such pretext to avoid feeling too bad. In brief, I could not go to sleep because of the numerous girlie photographs in these magazines; the nude photographs of young ladies —these fascinating photographs which have been slowly firing my imagination. I was absorbed in fantasies for one or two hours, looking over these obscene photographs. While I was appreciating these photos, the cocks crowed, those town criers of day-break, a bean-curd peddler passed, and finally a garbage-truck came to the entrance of our building to sweep away the American girls from my tired imagination, with much other trash. What is left is this yawn. *(Opens his mouth wide.)* There is another reason to buy these magazines. Yesterday, Saturday, I went to a movie. One of the ideal pleasures of the world is that of men and women enjoying themselves together. God did have some reason in creating such a pair. And most other people went to see the movie together, in pairs, but I went alone—I haven't any girl to go with. The story of the movie concerned a passionate love. After seeing it, I felt something awfully strange. So, I wandered all about Chong-no street by myself, and then I found myself being pushed into the crowd on the Myŏngdong streets, glancing at women's faces and bodies going to and from the Western dress shops. At last I came to the alley behind the Ch'ŏnil Bank to pick up these two copies of different American magazines. Hence I had no choice but to fantasize until 3 o'clock this morning, looking at these photos. *(Again he walks toward the room.)* I am still a bachelor. At the age of thirty-one I am aware that this is nothing to be proud of. But this is an inevitable true fact. I have had little chance to be with girls; I do not have enough courage to know and visit them. As a result, I cannot help myself; I can only buy those magazines.

Though sometimes I've had the chance, I did not have enough nerve. For example, this has been the case with Miss Pak living on the fourth floor.

(Pak Yong-ja, carrying a kimch'i* pot, enters from left of the stage and knocks on an imaginary door.)

(Sang-bŏm opens the door.)

Yong-ja: How are you, Mr. Kim?

Sang-bŏm: Just fine.

(Awkwardness between the two)

Yong-ja: Here. . . I brought some *kimch'i* for you. Since I heard that you cook for yourself. . . . My mother wanted me give you this. . . .

Sang-bŏm: . . . I don't know your mother well.

Yong-ja: Are you. . .? We live in apartment 43. My name is Pak Yong-ja.

Sang-bŏm: . . .Yes. I remember you well. I'm Kim Sang-bŏm. I saw you in church. You're in the choir, aren't you?

Yong-ja: Yes. I saw you in church also. So, take this *kimch'i* please. . . .

Sang-bŏm: (Accepting the kimch'i pot) Ah, thank you!. . .
(Though he has accepted the kimch'i pot, he is embarrassed with it.)

Yong-ja: Beautiful day! It's really like an autumn day, isn't it?

Sang-bŏm: Yes, it is. The weather's O.K., though it may be cloudy this afternoon, because a high-pressure system from Mongolia is resting over this area. . . .

Yong-ja: . . .Well, I have to go.

---

* *kimch'i:* A favorite Korean spicy dish, made of pickled vegetables, including cabbage radishes, turnips, peppers, and garlic, prepared by a fermentation process.

Sang-bŏm: Yes?

(*Yong-ja goes out.*)

Ah!. . .I say. . .I will enjoy this. . . .(*To the audience*) Yes! This is the way things worked out. I don't know why I had to talk about that high pressure system from Mongolia. In fact, fine weather simply meant that she wanted to come into my room and talk with me. How come the first conversation between a man and woman has to start with "beautiful weather, isn't it?" or "the weather's fine, isn't it?" All kinds of beautiful dialogue and gestures which I have designed, looking over those nude photographs, are frozen before a girl in reality. At any rate, thanks to this girl, Pak Yong-ja, living in apartment 43, once every week a *kimch'i* pot comes into my room.

Dear me! It's already close to eleven o'clock. I have to go to church. (*He takes his jacket and combs his hair.*)

In the alley just behind this apartment there is a church. About a month ago, I was so bored. . . . Well, I don't know why Sunday is so boring. . . at any rate, being so bored, I went to the church. The sound of the ladies' choir flowing from the church is lovely, isn't it?

And I went to the church, just to see the girls. Sitting in a rear seat, I formed the habit of appreciating the faces and bodies of the women sitting around me and the sweet young girls in the choir. Then, one day I happened to meet the president of my company. Well, I discovered he is an elder in this church. I wonder, does money always go with religion? The president welcomed me. He even praised me as a commendable member of his company. Being in a predicament, I became a forced Christian churchgoer. All of a sudden, the "hobby" of going to church to see girls changed into a "duty." When he asked me whether I came to church every Sunday, I told him that I'd been coming only sometimes. He wanted me to attend every Sunday. I had no choice. Indeed he is my benefactor. It is this very president who hired me as a probationary employee and promoted me to full-time regular employment. I came to know the president through this peculiar circumstance at the church. *(He produces toilet paper from his rear pocket and shows it to the audience.)*

This toilet paper has formed a connection between us. I say, this toilet paper with which we blow our nose or go to the restroom.

(Shafts of light are focused on the office, stage left. The business manager sits back against his arm-chair, reading the newspaper. Sang-bŏm takes a seat behind a small desk at his left. He uses his abacus and turns the papes of an account-book).

Yŏng-min: Mr. Kim! Do you have a cigarette?

Sang-bŏm: Cigarette? I don't know how to smoke.

Yŏng-min: You see one over there! Bring it to me, please.

Sang-bŏm: Yes, sir!

    (Sang-bŏm goes to the table and brings the cigarette to him. Yŏng-min accepts it and leisurely lights up.)

Yŏng-min: Though you don't smoke, at least you should be polite enough to suggest it to the smoker!

Sang-bŏm: I will remember it next time, sir!

Yŏng-min: What am I, *Sang-bŏm?*

Sang-bŏm: What?. . . You're the business manager.

Yŏng-min: What's my name?

Sang-bŏm: . . .Bae. . .manager Bae. Sir!

Yŏng-min: Hmph! There you are! Although you're only a probationary employee, at least you should know the name of your immediate boss. Listen! My name is Pae Yŏng-min.

Sang-bŏm: I will never forget it, sir!

Yŏng-min: Consider yourself lucky. I'm not disciplining you for this.

Sang-bŏm: *(A few minutes later)* Sir, did you serve in the army for a long time?

Yŏng-min: Yes, a pretty long time. I was discharged from the

army as a major.
(Sang-bŏm continues to work. A few minutes later Sŏng A-mi comes out from the president's office.)

A-mi: (*Sitting on the sofa*) Our president is depressed.

Yŏng-min: Why?

A-mi: He got a call from the Chong-no police station. One of our people got into a big fight in a bar. Some windows were smashed. . . the legs of a dinner table were broken. . . . The bar was totally destroyed. He's now chewing out the general manager on the phone because of it.

Yŏng-min: What's embarrassing is that our president is an elder in a church. . . .

A-mi: Ah, how disgraceful it is! Did you join them for drink, sir?

Yŏng-min: I joined them for a while early in the evening. Then I went home.
(The door flies open and the president bursts in, in a fury. But he doesn't say anything. He stalks about for a while and goes out. He's on his way to the restroom. Whenever he gets angry, he goes to the men's room.)

A-mi: Why did they drink so much like that? Instead of a curfew hour, there should be a liquor prohibition.

Yŏng-min: I say, agreed. If they drink wine moderately, it can be rather good for their health. . . .Mr. Kim, do you drink too?

Sang-bŏm: Hum? I don't know how to drink.

A-mi: Mr. Kim, didn't you go to the party last night?

Sang-bŏm: I am. . . not yet. . . qualified to participate in that kind of party, because I am only a probationary employee. . . .

Yŏng-min: Other than you, who else in the world calls himself only a probationary employee every time he speaks.

A-mi: If they hire a man, he should be a regular employee. What is this probationary employment anyway? Why do they want to make such a distinction. . .?

Yŏng-min: That kind of. . . probationary employment

system. . . (*Watching A-mi's expression*) . . . was created by the general manger, Pak.

Sang-bŏm: Was it the general manager's idea?

(*There is a change in A-mi's expression. She continues to work, clearing her throat. Then the president returns.*)

President: Hell, no toilet paper in our men's room? What is our company, only a bunch of drunkards? It's become chaos around here. Chaos!

Now tell me, why can't I find any toilet paper in our men's room?

(*Sang-bŏm stands and pulls out some toilet paper from his pocket and offers it to the president.*)

Sang-bŏm: This is only poor Korean-made toilet paper, though. . . .

(*President is about to go out, crunching it in his hand, but turns again.*)

President: I say. . . .

A-mi: Yes?

President: Call the general manager and tell him to fire this man named Yu Pong-il. He's in jail. He's a no-good lout. He lies around drunk all day long. He's the one who's spoiled the atmosphere of our company. He's stirring up one incident after another. This is one company that will not tolerate drunkards!

Yŏng-min: Sir!. . . Mr. Yu Pong-il is capable enough to have won a prize in the national abacus calculation contest. . . . He is one of the best interpreters of the regulations of the Department of Finance. If you forgive him once. . . .

President: (*To Sang-bŏm*) What did you say your name was?

Sang-bŏm: Yes, sir! (*He gathers himself and replies in a loud voice.*) I am a probationary employee, Kim Sang-bŏm, sir!

President: How much do you drink?

Sang-bŏm: I don't drink at all, sir!

President: (*To A-mi*) I say, tell them to promote this young man to regular employment in place of that drunkard.

(*The president goes out.*)

Sang-bŏm: (*He produces more toilet paper from his pocket and shows it to the audience.*) Now! You see? Thank Heaven! Because of this 5 *wŏn* worth of toilet paper, I have become a full-time regular employee of this company. Let me say, first, thanks to some of this toilet paper from the men's room, and second, thanks to my church-going to stare at the girls, I won the president's favor. "Life is unpredictable! Hope may rise even from despair." This is what one of my old home-room teachers used to tell us. Originally he loved literature. Now he has given up not only his teaching job but also literature.

And he is involved in a business selling *sŏllŏng-t'ang** soup. . . . Well, as he used to say life is unpredictable. . . . Who knows what may rise up from a miserable soup bowl? Last Sunday, I say, the president was even kind enough to visit this shabby room after church.

(*President comes in, carrying a Bible and hymn book together under his arm.*)

Sang-bŏm: Though my place is somewhat humble. . . please have a seat, sir!

President: All right. . . do you live alone?

Sang-bŏm: Yes, sir!

President: You mean you're not married?

Sang-bŏm: No, sir! Because I am living with the love of God, I am not lonely, sir!

President: Good boy!

Sang-bŏm: Would you like a cup of coffee. . . sir?

President: I don't smoke.

Sang-bŏm: Sir?

President: I don't smoke. What about you?

Sang-bŏm: I. . .drink. . . .

President: Drink?. . . Oh, you're talking about coffee! I thought you were talking about tobacco. Don't bother with it. Soon I have to leave. By the way, where are you

---

* sŏllŏng-t'ang: a kind of beef bouillon with rice, a popular Korean dish.

from?

Sang-bŏm: Seoul, sir!

President: Then, why do you live here?

Sang-bŏm: My house is in Ch'angsin-dong. But I want to live an independent life. . . .

President: Both of your parents are alive. . .?

Sang-bŏm: Yes, sir!

President: What does your father do, Sang-bŏm?

Sang-bŏm: Yes, my father. . . tells fortunes.

President: Fortunetelling?

Sang-bŏm: Yes, sir! There is a fortuneteller's house called "the Turtle House" on the hill in Ch'angsin-dong. It's run by my father.

President: . . .Ah, your father tells fortunes. Do you have brothers?

Sang-bŏm: Yes, sir! My eldest brother is a professor of engineering at a university in Inch'ŏn. He tells me he's doing research on rockets.

President: Rockets? What kind of rocket research is there in Korea? He must be a college professor.

Sang-bŏm: Yes, he is, sir!

President: And then. . . ?

Sang-bŏm: My second brother was killed, sir!

President: Oh my God! That's too bad. Indeed, life and death depend upon Heaven. I also lost my only son! Just six months ago. He died six months after he married. Miss Sŏng, working in my office, is my daughter-in-law. Even though my son died, she still helps me. It's God's will.

Sang-bŏm: My second brother was killed by accident. A shotgun misfired.

President: A shotgun?

Sang-bŏm: Yes, sir! He was really crazy about hunting.

President: Ha! I like hunting also. Hunting is not killing. . . but good exercise. Indeed, it is a sport.

Sang-bŏm: I agree, sir! Would you like to see the shotgun which my brother used?

President: You have the shotgun here?

Sang-bŏm: Yes, sir! *(Sang-bŏm enters the room at stage left and brings out a shotgun.)* This is the gun, sir.

President: Ah! *(He stands holding the shotgun and aiming it stylishly.)* Though it's a little rusty, it seems a good gun. It's made in the U.S.A.?

Sang-bŏm: Yes, sir! He bought it from a G.I., sir.

President: This is all right, though mine is Belgian, you know.

Sang-bŏm: Bug? Sir!

President: I tell you, the best shotguns are made in Belgium. Sang-bŏm, do you know how to use a shotgun?

Sang-bŏm: I've shot it once or twice but still I'm very poor. . . .

President: Do you know how to take care of it?

Sang-bŏm: Yes, sir! Because caring for it is a simple thing. . . .

President: I have a shotgun in my office. I want you to come from time to time and keep it in good shape.

Sang-bŏm: Yes, I will remember, sir.

President: The shotgun is only for shooting animals, how did it come to shoot a man! . . . You told me that your second brother was killed that way. . . don't you have any other brothers?

Sang-bŏm: I'm the next brother, sir. And after me there's one more brother. He's now preparing to find a job. After he graduated from junior college, he took the entrance exams at several companies. But. . . he still hasn't passed. . . .

President: If he works hard, he will make it. All your brothers are Christian, I suppose?

Sang-bŏm: Sir?

President: I say, all of your brothers believe in God?

Sang-bŏm: No. . . sir. I am the only one. . . .

President: (Standing up) Why don't you encourage them to go to church? If they go to church many things can. . . you know what I mean, Sang-bŏm! First of all, church teaches the virtue of self-sacrifice. A self-sacrificing spirit is important for all human beings. Speaking of self-sacrifice, I want to know how you feel about the atmosphere in our company.

Sang-bŏm: Well, I don't know, sir.

President: Any complaints among our people?

Sang-bŏm: I don't know, sir.

President: If there are any complaints or other things I can't detect, please let me know as soon as possible. The best way you can help me is to keep me informed about that kind of thing. It's sort of service-spirit, isn't it? Now tell me, have you seen any other drinkers in the office?

Sang-bŏm: I'll keep my eyes open, sir.

President: Well, I'm going.

    (He walks out the imaginary door and exits stage left. Sang-bŏm makes a low bow to him from the middle of stage.)

Sang-bŏm: The president has made me into a spy. I feel a little ashamed. But this is my only chance for success in life. So far I have had my troubles in school, in society. . . I'm afraid my future will be nothing but troubles. In my college days I left home and cooked for myself. At that time, clutching my stomach, I studied all night long. But my friends spent only an hour or so preparing their material to cheat in the exams and then went to sleep. Their grades were far better than mine. I found a job in a steel factory in Inch'ŏn, but after two years I was fired. I was involved in a demonstration against the merger of two steel factories. My president and general manager ordered me to do it. The general manager forced me to hold a placard at the front of our rally, and I did as he wanted. Afterwards I was beaten by demonstrators from the other side. I was knocked cold. When I opened my eyes I found myself in jail. I was branded as the main agitator of the demonstration! Insisting I could not be, I tried to straighten things out with them, but the president requested me to leave his factory. He said that it was not the time to make things clear. After that, I was forced to come to Seoul and become a probationary employee in this company. That's my past

. . . . Even though I've become a full-time regular staff member and taken a room in this building, the trouble from other people is just about the same as before. I've never tried to profit by inflicting trouble on other people. I say, I don't know why I should have been in trouble like this. There's a man living in the next room. I don't know what he does. But sometimes I see girls coming to his room. Sometimes they sleep with him. There's nothing except a large bed in his room. So far I've never seen him go out to work in the morning. This fellow also causes me trouble.

(Tank comes out and knocks on Sang-bŏm's door.) Come in, please.

(Tank comes in.)

Tank: Why don't we get to know each other? I live just next door to you.

Sang-bŏm: Yes, my name is Kim Sang-bŏm. Please have a seat.

Tank: What company do you work for?

Sang-bŏm: It's a steel company on Chong-no.

Tank: A steel company?

Sang-bŏm: A place where steel. . . iron is made.

Tank: Oh! A steel mill! I know what you mean. I'm just here to get a light.

(Hyŏn So-hi comes in dressed only in a night gown. She looks sleepy. A cigarette dangles from her lips.)

So-hi: Did you get a light?

Sang-bŏm: My name is Kim Sang-bŏm.

So-hi: Hi! I'm Miss Hyŏn. My first name is So-hi.

Tank: I say, a lighter please, if you have it.

Sang-bŏm: Yes, I have.

(He takes a lighter from his pocket and flicks it. Tank and So-hi light their cigarettes from it.)

So-hi: Thank you.

Tank: Here, have a cigarette.

Sang-bŏm: I don't smoke.

Tank: Oh? What do you carry a lighter for?

So-hi: Tank!

Tank: Yeah?

Sang-bŏm: You're called Tank?

So-hi: This guy's name is Tank.

    (*Sang-bŏm laughs in a loud voice.*)

Tank: Yea, my name is Tank. But what do you want?

So-hi: Whether he carries a lighter or not, what's it to you? Don't waste time.

Tank: You know, you're not a bad looking fellow! I say, . . . what did you say your name was?

Sang-bŏm: Kim Sang-bŏm.

Tank: Mr. Kim! I'm sorry to ask. . . by any chance. . . do you happen to have some coffee?

Sang-bŏm: Coffee?

Tank: Since I drank a bit last night, I have an unpleasant taste in my mouth.

Sang-bŏm: Yes. . . I may have some coffee. I may have some coffee in the kitchen which I left boiling this morning. . . .

Tank: If I may ask, please lend me the pot too, so that we can make a little for ourselves.

Sang-bŏm: . . . By all means. (*Sang-bŏm walks into the kitchen. Tank makes a curious gesture to So-hi showing that he is the greatest in the world. Looking through the magazines scattered on the couch, So-hi compares her figure with the nude photographs in it. Sang-bŏm brings out his coffee-pot.*)

Tank: Ah! Thanks. We'll be seeing you often.

So-hi: Tank, do you have sugar?

Tank: Ah! I forgot, Mr. Kim. Please lend me some sugar.

Sang-bŏm: Sure.

    (*He again enters the kitchen and brings out a box of sugar to give So-hi.*)

So-hi: Do you live alone?

Sang-bŏm: Yes, I live alone.

So-hi: . . . Don't you have a chick?

Sang-bŏm: (*Shamefully*) Ah. . . I don't.

(In his embarrassment, he takes away the magazines.)

So-hi: Thanks a lot.

(Tank and So-hi step out together, looking like lovers.)

Sang-bŏm: (To the audience) You see? I am always troubled like this. Not only do that strange man, Tank, living next door, and his mistress, So-hi, bother me, but the manager of this building does the same thing. Even at night I can't be safe from this kind of nuisance.

(The manager, drunk, knocks on Sang-bŏm's door, and enters his room.)

Manager: Ah, Mr. Sang-bŏm! You're not asleep yet.

Sang-bŏm: I was asleep, but your knock woke me up.

Manager: Ah, is that right? Life is short. How is it you can sleep when life is so short? *(In a sentimental tone)* "To close your eyes is to die, to open your eyes is to live." Do you know whose saying that is?

Sang-bŏm: No. I don't know much about literature. . . . Who said it?

Manager: I said it. I, the manager of this building! That is what this manager said. You have a pocket notebook?

Sang-bŏm: Notebook? What do you mean by that? You mean, like this?

Manager: Yes, if you have a pocket notebook, please jot down my words. If you record my words once a day, you'll make a greater book than the Bible in five years. Because I always speak the truth.

Sang-bŏm: You must be very drunk. You look it.

Manager: Drunk? Yes, I am drunk! I say life is too tedious not to be drunk. If it weren't for drink, what kind of entertainment would I have to live for? When I return home, what's waiting for me is that. . . my wife and the six dull faces of her clinging relatives. Twenty years. . . we've been married twenty years and we still don't have a child, not one! Perhaps it's my fault. My wife insists that it's not her fault. Nevertheless. . . with no child of my own, why should I feed six of my in-laws? But that's how it is, down it! It's my fate!

Sang-bŏm: You're too drunk. Not long ago you were in the hospital because of your heart. . . . You should be careful.

Manager: I wish I could have another heart attack—and die this time. It's what I am, a goddamn hotel manager.

Sang-bŏm: Please go to your wife. She's waiting for you.

Manager: She is not waiting for me. What she waits for is the money—the money to feed her own family, her relatives. Let me sleep here, please. Today Mr. Sang-bŏm is the manager, I am his guest! *(He takes out money from an inner pocket.)* This is 50 thousand *wŏn!* I earned this money with great difficulty. Please take care of this for me. If I take this home, my wife will surely snatch it away immediately.

Sang-bŏm: Listen, don't be like this. . . .

Manager: You're my buddy. Why don't you accept a request from a buddy? It is not too difficult to let me sleep here and to keep this money for me. Please hold onto the money for me for a while! You are my buddy, aren't you? Sure you are! Buddy!

Indeed! Friendship, that's very complicated. You can maintain a good friendship with a man only if you remain detached from him. If you get too close to him, he may turn out to be an enemy. The meaning of "friend" is not "close" but "distant." Those people with whom you make friends, if you keep you distance, they'll become true friends. If you get too close, your friendship will break up easily. Moreover, friends are a stupid thing! To make them happy, you have to always be praising them. If you blame them, they forsake you. Those fellows are happy only when you praise them. Otherwise, they forsake you. In Korea a friend is a burden, a strain on your mind.

If you make friends, keep them at a distance. At a distance, I say! Well. . . shall I call my wife? No, she's probably not even waiting up for me. Forget about it. Let me go to sleep.

(Sang-bŏm walks into the bedroom, supporting the manager by his arm. A few minutes later he comes out again, panting, sweating heavily. He picks up a money bag from the tea table and turns to the audience.)

Sang-bŏm: Even this money bag I have to take care of. . . . By all means I should get married. Since I live alone, people try to take advantage of me in many ways. I have nearly no money for marriage, but Miss Pak on the third floor shows some special kindness to me. What's more, her mother, Mrs. Mun, does too.

(Mrs. Mun enters the room carrying a kimch'i pot.)

Mrs. Mun: Ah, I'm glad to see you're here!

Sang-bŏm: How are you, Mrs. Mun?

Mrs. Mun: Here's some *kimch'i*. This time my daughter herself prepared it. My daughter looks cute, aristocratic, don't you think? She's a smart one, all right, and oh, how she can cook! She is working hard. I say, what do you think about my daughter's skin? Really white, isn't it?

Sang-bŏm: Yes. I suppose it is.

Mrs. Mun: Ah, the other day when we went to a public bath, all the other people stared at her. What soft, white skin my daughter has!

Sang-bŏm: . . . Yeah. . . .

Mrs. Mun: This time she added some raw chestnut and ginger to the *kimch'i*. Well, I'd better go now. I forgot something! I take it you're free tonight?

Sang-bŏm: Yes, Mam.

(Mrs. Mun exits.)

Yong-ja's mother seems to like me, doesn't she? Sometimes she and her mother appear in my dream as a pair of chopsticks. Yes, Miss Pak and her mother have been transformed into two chopsticks that try to pick me up like this. *(He holds up two fingers to the audience.)* Miss Pak gets close enough to me to enter my room even in the night.

(Pak Yong-ja knocks on the imaginary door and enters the room.)

Yong-ja: I have some roast chestnuts for you. Do you like chestnuts?

Sang-bŏm: What I like the most is steamed bread, but roast chestnuts will be all right. Have a seat, please.
(*Young-ja sits and peels the roast chestnuts.*) Did you buy these on the street?

Yong-ja: No. I found some chestnuts at home and roasted them for you.
(*Yong-ja peels the chestnuts and gives them to Sang-bŏm.*)

Sang-bŏm: I'm O.K.!

Yong-ja: Please take this!

Sang-bŏm: No, you take them. I'm O.K.

Yong-ja: Oh, dear me! Please take them.
(*Sang-bŏm eats a roast chestnut, awkwardly, with his fingers.*)
Isn't it sweet?

Sang-bŏm: It's not well done, but sweet enough.

Yong-ja: I say. . . . Are you busy tonight?

Sang-bŏm: No, I'm not.

Yong-ja: Then let's go see a movie. We can go to a movie.
My mother got three tickets somewhere.

Sang-bŏm: What kind of movie is it?

Yong-ja: I have no idea. My mother bought the tickets. She's coming here soon. She's changing her clothes.

Sang-bŏm: Is this movie really interesting?

Yong-ja: Well, who knows?
(*Sang-bŏm takes a coin from his pocket.*)

Sang-bŏm: This coin is worth five *wŏn*. I'm telling our fortune with this. I can tell whether this movie is interesting or not by tossing this coin. (*Sang-bŏm flips the coin, catches it in his palm, looks at it.*) Ah! It's heads. The movie will be interesting.

Yong-ja: How can you tell a fortune correctly with such a poor method?

Sang-bŏm: It always tells the truth. My father tells fortunes philosophically. But I do it with this coin. Sometimes I do it. . . .

(At this time Kim Sang-hak turns away at stage left and knocks on the imaginary door.) You have come too soon. *(Yong-ja stands up to open the door. Sang-hak enters the room.)*

Oh, dear me!

Sang-hak: Thank you.

Sang-bŏm: Ah, brother!

Sang-hak: Ah, I am glad to see you at home.

Sang-bŏm: When did you come from Inch'ŏn?

Sang-hak: I took the evening train. Because tomorrow is the anniversary of our university's founding. I got two days off.

Sang-bŏm: Ah, Miss Pak. This is my elder brother. He's teaching at a university in Inch'ŏn.

Sang-hak: Glad to know you. My name is Sang-hak.

Yong-ja: My. . . my name is Pak Yong-ja.

Sang-hak: Since things are a little dull in Inch'ŏn these days, I want to see my brother. . . .

Sang-bŏm: Brother, did you eat supper?

Sang-hak: Yes, I had supper in Inch'ŏn.

Yong-ja: Then, a cup of coffee?

Sang-bŏm: Right.

Yong-ja: I'll make coffee.

Sang-bŏm: No, let me do it. . . .

Yong-ja: You just enjoy talking together.

(Yong-ja exits stage left.)

Sang-hak: This is too bad, I am sorry. . . . If I'd known you were with your girl, I wouldn't have come. . . .

Sang-bŏm: Oh, no! She lives on the third floor. . . . I have nothing to do with her. She said she's going to see a movie. Well, how's it going?

Sang-hak: The same as usual. . . .

Sang-bŏm: Are you still working on rockets?

Sang-hak: I completed the second phase shooting. . . . But because of the damn research funds. . . .

(Mrs. Mun, Yong-ja's mother, comes and knocks on his door.)

Mrs. Mun: Oh, no! . . . Where is my daughter. . . ?

Sang-bŏm: Please come in. She's in the kitchen.

Mrs. Mun: Is she?

Sang-bŏm: Yes, she's making coffee. . . .

Mrs. Mun: . . . Ah. . . since she's reached the marriageable age, she should learn to do kitchen chores.

Sang-bŏm: This is my brother. He's a college professor in In-ch'ŏn. This is Miss Pak's mother.

Sang-hak: Glad to meet you. I am Kim Sang-hak.

Mrs. Mun: Yes. . . . What a smart man! All your brothers are. . . .

(Yong-ja comes out.)

Yong-ja: The coffee will be ready, soon. I say, what's the title of the movie, mother?

Mrs. Mun: (Taking out the tickets from her handbag) Ah. . . are these. . . .

Yong-ja: (She snatches the tickets from her mother and reads one.)

Apartment.

Sang-bŏm: "Apartment?" I saw that movie last Saturday. It's a good movie. Jack Lemmon's in it, playing the fool.

Mrs. Mun: (Discouraged) You saw the movie already?

Sang-bŏm: Well, I say, brother, did you see this movie? . . .

Sang-hak: Me? When did I have time to see it?

Sang-bŏm: (To Mrs. Mun) I can't see the same movie twice, can I? My elder brother hasn't seen it. Would you mind going to see the movie with him?

Mrs. Mun: . . . O.K. If you saw it already. . . . *(with reluctance to Sang-hak)* Please come. . . with us.

Sang-bŏm: Good. Well then, after enjoying the movie, please come back here, brother. You stay with me tonight. Miss Pak, you go ahead with my brother.

Yong-ja: . . . Yes.

Sang-hak: Well, shall we go now?

(Three people exeunt. Sang-hak returns.)

Sang-hak: I have a few hundred *wŏn* with me. . . but. . . who knows, something may happen. If you have money, give me a few hundred.

Sang-bŏm: I think I have some money.

(He gives his brother a few hundred wŏn after feeling in his pocket.)

Sang-hak: Well! I'll see you after the movie. Is this movie good?

Sang-bŏm: Ah, it's very interesting.

(Sang-hak walks out.)

(To the audience) That night when my elder brother came back from the movie, I gave him some wine, which I don't usually drink myself. My elder brother is 35 years old, he is not married, partly because he's been busy with his work. . . and partly because he doesn't have the money to marry.

It will be a little sad if I marry Miss Pak before he gets married. . . but from every point of view, I've thought, it would be better for me to get married. And I've started to save money little by little. From something in the way, she talks, I think she's put aside a considerable amount of money for her marriage.

About one month after that evening, my brother visited me again, this time with our younger brother, Sang-ch'ŏl.

(Sang-hak and Sang-ch'ŏl enter the room and sit on the couch.)

Sang-bŏm: Well, are you ready for your exam?

Sang-ch'ŏl: I sleep only five hours a night. I pour all my time into my studies. Yet too many people have applied, I'm afraid. . . .

Sang-hak: In case that company does hire you, what's the salary?

Sang-ch'ŏl: I don't know. Is that important? What is important is that I pass the examination and find a job.

Sang-hak: Yes, you'll be relieved if you pass that exam.

Sang-ch'ŏl: But then what do I do? Do you know any other way to find a job?

Sang-bŏm: Well, this time do you expect to pass?

Sang-ch'ŏl: According to Father's predictions, I have a good possibility to pass.

Sang-bŏm: Our Father's fortunetelling? Don't be silly. Father's fortunetelling is his job. You don't realize that yet?

Sang-ch'ŏl: Indeed, the number of people who come to see Father has drastically decreased.

Sang-hak: How could a fortuneteller's son be successful in rocket research?

Sang-bŏm: We didn't come here to discuss this, but. . . a month from now will be Father's sixty-first birthday.

Sang-hak: Sixty-first birthday? He's that old already?

Sang-bŏm: Time flies. . . .

Sang-ch'ŏl: Well, the three of us must have a talk about Father's birthday.

Sang-bŏm: I think so. Now that most of his friends have passed on. . . .

Sang-ch'ŏl: According to Mother's estimate, 30 thousand *wŏn* will be needed to celebrate his birthday.

Sang-bŏm: Thirty thousand *wŏn?*

Sang-ch'ŏl: That's a minimum amount they say.

Sang-hak: Well. . . after taking out the miscellaneous items, only one thousand is left from my salary. Take out the boarding house expenses and only 500 is left!

Sang-bŏm: The salary of a nobody at the bottom like me is even more meager. . . .

Sang-ch'ŏl: We can send invitation cards to our friends. If about a hundred people come, we can collect 30 thousand, if we figure on 300 *wŏn* per person. . . .

Sang-hak: Friends? A hundred? Don't talk so foolishly.

Sang-bŏm: What other choice do we have?

Sang-hak: Well. . . .

(*An awkward silence follows.*)

Sang-ch'ŏl: Brothers, did you listen to the boxing match on the radio between Yun Kang-jŏn and Saruma last?

Sang-bŏm: I didn't.

Sang-ch'ŏl: It was really amazing.

Sang-hak: I listened to it at home. Saruma was down in the seventh round, wasn't he?

Sang-ch'ŏl: Ah! Yun Kang-jŏn was tough, really tough.

Sang-hak: It's a miracle that Korea has produced such a champion. . . .

Sang-bŏm: He's said to be only 19 years old! Is that true?

Sang-ch'ŏl: No, 22 years old.

Sang-hak: In our school there is one boxer, . . . he said that Kang is 22 years old.

Sang-bŏm: Our business manager is a boxing fanatic. He said Kang is 19 years old.

Sang-ch'ŏl: You're both wrong. He is twenty years old. I saw it in a newspaper story about the fight.

Sang-hak: I was told one of my students practiced boxing with Yun Kang-jŏn. Surely he must be 22.

Sang-ch'ŏl: Indeed! I've never missed a boxing match on the radio. . . . I insist Yun Kang-jŏn is 20 years old.

(*Another awkward silence*)

This year a Vietnamese girl became Miss Universe.

Sang-bŏm: I thought she was a Thai girl.

Sang-hak: Whether she is a Vietnamese or a Thai, she must be Oriental. There days the Oriental girls can beat the Western women!

Sang-ch'ŏl: Why?

Sang-hak: What. . . bosom. . . .

Sang-ch'ŏl: What?

Sang-hak: Ah, this. . . (*pointing at his own breast*). . . I am talking about this.

Sang-ch'ŏl: Ah, the breast!

Sang-hak: Right. The size of it is 36 inches around.

Sang-bŏm: No, it's 35 inches. I read it in the papers.

Sang-hak: I saw it in TIME magazine. 35 inches, it said.

Sang-ch'ŏl: Both of you are wrong. It's 38 inches.

Sang-hak: 38 inches? Are you crazy? Do you know how big that is, 38 inches?

Sang-ch'ŏl: That's why she became Miss Universe.

Sang-bŏm: Perhaps it's 35 inches.

Sang-ch'ŏl: I said no! It's 38 inches.

Sang-hak: You are obsessed with the 38th parallel. That's why you say so. Perhaps it's really 37 inches.

Sang-ch'ŏl: I said 38 inches.

　　(Another awkward silence)

　　. . . I say. . . think about what we can do for Father's birthday. Where can we get 30 thousand?

Sang-hak: Well. . . . It's quite late. Shall we go home?

Sang-ch'ŏl: When can we get together again?

Sang-bŏm: Well. . . .

　　(Sang-hak stands up and walks toward the door.)

Sang-hak: I say, let's go home.

　　(Sang-ch'ŏl also stands up and follows his brother.)

　　Hey, Sang-ch'ŏl, you go ahead and wait for me outside. I have something to talk over with Sang-bŏm.

Sang-ch'ŏl: O.K.! Goodbye, Sang-bŏm.

　　(Sang-ch'ŏl goes out.)

Sang-hak: I say, we have to celebrate Father's birthday, and

　　. . . .

Sang-bŏm: Right, it's really a big problem.

Sang-hak: I. . . I may get married within about a month.

Sang-bŏm: What? Marriage? Ah, congratulations! You should have married earlier. . . . I also intend to get married. But it would be a little bit awkward to get married earlier than you do. . . . Now everything's worked out just fine.

Sang-hak: That's why I'm telling you. I'd like to invite some guests to Father's birthday, but since my wedding will take place about a month after Father's birthday, I couldn't invite the same guests twice. . . .

Sang-bŏm: I'm afraid you're right. . . .

Sang-hak: Since it's this way, I want you to take the responsibility for celebrating Father's birthday.

Sang-bŏm: I understand what you mean. I'll talk to my boss about our difficult situation. . . .

Sang-hak: Please do as you like.

Sang-bŏm: By the way, what kind of girl are you going to marry?

Sang-hak: You know the girl very well.

Sang-bŏm: Me?

Sang-hak: I'm talking about the Miss Pak who lives upstairs. Because I found she is good enough as a housekeeper. . . .

Sang-bŏm: What, are you talking about Pak Yong-ja?

Sang-hak: Right. You have no objection, I hope.

Sang-bŏm: Me?. . . oh,. . . no. . . .

Sang-hak: (Looking at his watch) Oh, dear! I'm in danger of being late! Well, then, I'll be in touch with you in the next two or three days.

Sang-bŏm: Has she agreed to marry you?

Sang-hak: Of course. She came down to Inch'ŏn to visit me a few times. We've decided to skip the engagement. We've also decided to have a very simple wedding. It was because we went to the movie on that night that we've gotten together now. Well, so long. . . .

(*Sang-hak steps out. Sang-bŏm cannot move for a while. He roots himself where he stands.*)

Sang-bŏm: (Showing regret rather than resignation toward the apparent loss of Yong-ja)

Oh dear!. . . What a fate!. . . I'm destined not only to be deprived of my bride but to pay the expense for Father's birthday. I'm at a loss for words. I'm 31. I have at most about 20 years to go. . . . When I think about living with pain like this for another twenty years, my head reels. . . .

Up till now I've always acted correctly, I've lived within the boundaries of common sense.

When I was in Inch'ŏn something very strange happened. It was such a hot summer day that I went to the beach. From a distance I saw a fully-dressed young lady throwing herself into the water from a rock, and thought it must be a suicide. Tossing aside my straw hat I ran to save her from drowning. I couldn't understand why such a beautiful young girl would want to kill herself. When I pulled her onto the sand, she slapped my cheek instead of saying "Thank you." Then a policeman arrested me and put me in jail. So you see, my kind of common sense has become useless in this society. From now on, I know I should tie a heavy stone to someone who's drowning. Instead of offering my seat on the bus, I will cruelly kick aside anyone who stands in my path. Not only will I shun common sense, I'll ignore conventional morality as well. . . .

First I'll apply a new kind of common sense at my company.

(The office, stage left, lights up. Sŏng A-mi is fixing her make-up on the sofa. Sang-bŏm brings out a shotgun and beings cleaning it.)

A-mi: Be careful with that. You've taken all the shells out, I hope?

Sang-bŏm: Yes, I unloaded it.

A-mi: Do you go hunting very often?

Sang-bŏm: When the president goes hunting, sometimes I go with him.

A-mi: Are you . . . still single?

Sang-bŏm: I still haven't been able to get married. . . . By the way, aren't you going to re-marry?

A-mi: Me?. . . It's been only eight months since my husband died.

Sang-bŏm: You're talking about our president's son, aren't you?

A-mi: Don't make me sad by making me talk about my marriage.

I still cannot forget him.

Sang-bŏm: I'm sorry. I won't do it again.

(The telephone rings. Sang-bŏm answers it, still holding the shotgun.) Yes? Who? You're looking for Sŏng A-mi? Yes, ‸he's here. *(He thrusts the shotgun at her instead of the*

phone.) It's general manager Pae. Ah! I'm sorry. *(He gives her the phone.)*

A-mi: Yes, it's me. Him? He's an accountant, Mr. Kim Sangbŏm. No, no problems. . . . What? Right now? The president is still in his office. . . yes, I know. And then? Don't make me wait alone, please. . . .

　　(She hangs up and looks at her watch. She glances at Sang-bŏm. Then she steps into the president's office.)

Sang-bŏm: *(To the audience)* A minute ago she was saying she couldn't forget her husband who died eight months ago. When general manager Pae calls, she's ready to go out with him. Now, from my own common sense view, such a thing couldn't possibly happen. But I also have to live with the common sense of these other people, what I call the NEW COMMON SENSE.

　　(A-mi comes out from the president's office and exits stage left, carrying her handbag. Sang-bŏm aims the muzzle of the shotgun at her back. The door opens and the president comes out. Sang-bŏm turns and in an accidental reflex points the gun at the president.)

President: Come on now, boy!

Sang-bŏm: Ah! I'm very sorry. Now that I've cleaned it, suddenly I feel like firing it. . . .

President: *(Taking the gun and looking it over)* Yes, good work! Where's our business manager, Mr. Pae?

Sang-bŏm: Manager went to the Basket tea room with five thousand *wŏn*.

President: Five thousand? Not company money?

Sang-bŏm: Yes. He ordered me to give him five thousand, sir. . . .

President: And why did he have to go to the tea room during business hours?

Sang-bŏm: *(Reluctantly)* It seems. . . a woman is waiting for him. . . and. . . a while ago Miss Sŏng, the secretary, was here. . . .

President: She told me she had to see a dentist for a toothache. . . . Does manager Pae often draw his salary in advance?

Sang-bŏm: Well. . . . Since he sometimes used to draw out money without giving his signature. . . I don't know whether it's loan or not.

President: You keep a record of every *wŏn* manager Pae draws out!

Sang-bŏm: Yes, sir. . . . I will calculate exactly how much he's got.

President: Is this woman waiting in the tea room a callgirl?

Sang-bŏm: I have no idea, sir. But. . . .

President: But. . .?

Sang-bŏm: Manager Pae really loves wine. Sometimes he actually drinks wine even at lunch time.

President: How can he behave like that? He is in charge of the finances of this company. . . .

Sang-bŏm: Sir, I. . . don't. . . . I say such a thing only to you. . . just because I respect you and. . . simply I want to see this company prosper more than any other person. . . and I report this thing to you. I'm following the instructions which you gave me at church. . . .

President: I know it. I understand you, boy. Keep up the good work.

(*The president goes into his office with his gun. Sang-bŏm begins to work behind his desk. A few minutes later, Pae Yŏng-min comes in.*)

Yŏng-min: Anything happen while I was out?

Sang-bŏm: No, sir.

(*When Sang-bŏm sees Yŏng-min looking for a cigarette, he picks it up nimbly from the table, gives it to him, and lights it for him.*)

Yŏng-min: The president is in?

Sang-bŏm: Yes, he seems to be in.

Yŏng-min: Ah, I can't bear my damn wife's "urgent requests!" She forced me to lend five thousand *wŏn* to her friend who's in the hospital with appendicitis.

Sang-bŏm: You say. . . the lady who called you from the tea room a little while ago is. . . your wife?

Yŏng-min: Right. Housewives should not come to their husbands' offices. If they do come all they bring is trouble. It's highly embarrassing to meet them in the office. Their visits are bad omens, bad luck.

Sang-bŏm: (To the audience) Yes, he is unfortunate! Really unfortunate. About a month after this trouble, the business manager was forced to transfer to a branch in poor, rocky Kangwŏn Province and I took his place. All the people at the office are surprised that I have risen so fast.

This is the first result of giving up my original common sense and taking on the new common sense.

I have one more thing to do. It is to take advantage of the relationship between the widow, Sŏng A-mi, the president's daughter-in-law, and secretary; and general manager Pae. Thus I will open all possible doors for my rise in the world with these my own hands, and kick them open with these two feet.

(The office light turns out, the apartment interior lights up. Sang-bŏm comes in and fastens a big cross on the wall. Mrs. Mun arrives and knocks on the door. Sang-bŏm opens it.)

Sang-bŏm: Ah, how are you, Mrs. Mun?

Mrs. Mun: Glad to see you here. Ah, I've been so forgetful! I've been so busy making preparations for my daughter's marriage, I haven't had time to pickle *kimch'i* for you.

Sang-bŏm: No problem. I understand you must be very busy these days.

Mrs. Mun: You don't know yet?

Sang-bŏm: What do you mean?

Mrs. Mun: Ah! They say, our building manager died this evening.

Sang-bŏm: Really? The manager died?

Mrs. Mun: He had a weak heart, you know. . . .

Sang-bŏm: Another heart attack, you mean. . . .

Mrs. Mun: Yes, he died of heart failure. That's so sad. He's left a large family to support. . . . So I'm thinking of collecting some money from all tenants to show our sympathy for his bereaved family. . . .

Sang-bŏm: That's a good idea.

Mrs. Mun: As soon as you're free, please see me in my room tomorrow morning.

Sang-bŏm: Yes, I will.

(*Mrs. Mun is going out.*) I say. . . how did he die?

Mrs. Mun: They say he collapsed and died immediately while eating his supper.

Sang-bŏm: Without leaving any. . . . He didn't leave a will?

Mrs. Mun: Don't talk about a will. One moment he was alive and hearty, the next he was dead.

Sang-bŏm: Is that so! Then, I'll see you tomorrow morning.

Mrs. Mun: I still have many tenants to visit.

(*Mrs. Mun goes out. From under the sofa Sang-bŏm removes the money bag which the manager left in his care.*) (*To the audience*) This money! Fifty thousand! This is the precious property which the late manager entrusted to me. Well, what should I do with this money? Since he collapsed during dinner, it's almost certain he didn't have a will. Yes, he asked me to keep this money secret. It's impossible that he told anyone about this money. . . .

By my old common sense I should return this to his widow, but. . . no, now that I've abandoned my old common sense and am living by A NEW COMMON SENSE, it is not necessary to return the money because from the beginning he hated his wife. Me, he rather liked. Therefore, I'd better keep this money for myself. This logic is irresistible.

(*To the audience again*) So, I will use this money for myself. Now, the next day I met my younger brother in a downtown tea room. You know, my younger brother, the one who's preparing for the entrance exams at that company with the peculiar name.

(Sang-ch'ŏl brings in a chair and takes his seat at stage left front. Hyŏn So-hi brings in a small tea-table.)

So-hi: What kind of tea would you like?

Sang-ch'ŏl: . . . I say, I'm waiting for a man. I'd like to take my tea with him when he gets here.

So-hi: Sure.

(So-hi goes in. Sang-ch'ŏl takes a book from his pocket and reads it, underlining with a pencil. A few minutes later, Sang-bŏm brings in a chair and sits down.)

Sang-bŏm: Have you been waiting a long time?

Sang-ch'ŏl: No.

Sang-bŏm: Even in the tea room, you have to study for this examination!

Sang-ch'ŏl: Yes, I have no choice.

Sang-bŏm: Have you taken tea?

Sang-ch'ŏl: If you hadn't come, I might be in trouble. I'm broken, all I've got in my pocket is two bus tickets. Well, why did you want me to come?

Sang-bŏm: *(He calls out, turning his body.)* Hey! Two cups of pine juice, please!

Sang-ch'ŏl: It's expensive, remember, 50 *wŏn* a cup. . . .

Sang-bŏm: No problem. I'm a business manager now.

Sang-ch'ŏl: What? You? A business manager? Terrific! How did it happen so fast?

Sang-bŏm: Our president took a liking to me. What's more, I've mastered the secret of how to get along in the world.

Sang-ch'ŏl: You must be making twice as much.

Sang-bŏm: Now, salary doesn't matter. . . brother! Let me tell you. Now if you want to pass this so-called entrance examination. . . I suggest you make some behind-the-scenes efforts.

Sang-ch'ŏl: What kind of efforts?

Sang-bŏm: You may have to spend a little money? You must know that the world's like that.

(He pulls out some money from his inner pocket and places it in Sang-ch'ŏl's hand.) I say, this is five

thousand. . . .

Sang-ch'ŏl: What, five thousand?

Sang-bŏm: Give them some money. The world is not so simple as you think. The important thing is to get inside the door. It doesn't matter whether you get in through the front door or the rear door. Once you're inside, however you get there, then there will be no problems.

Sang-ch'ŏl: Oh, no. . . . I don't think I have the nerve for that. Who should I give the money to? How do I do it?

Sang-bŏm: That's your problem. Think about it, Sang-ch'ŏl.

Sang-ch'ŏl: (Putting the money back on the table) This will make things even more complicated. I'm busy enough studying for the entrance test. If I have to do that sort of thing too, things may become terribly complicated.

Sang-bŏm: I say, don't study hard. Then you'll have time to do it!

Sang-ch'ŏl: But. . . how can I take the exam without studying? Brother!

Sang-bŏm: You're burying your head in the sand! Be realistic! You need a NEW COMMON SENSE! I say, A NEW COMMON SENSE!

Sang-ch'ŏl: What?

Sang-bŏm: Forget about it, forget about it!

(Hyŏn So-hi comes out, carrying two glasses of juice.)

So-hi: Oh, my! Look at this money! Money all over the place. . . .

Sang-ch'ŏl: That belongs to my elder brother! Don't touch it.

So-hi: . . . This gentleman. . . . I saw him somewhere?

Sang-bŏm: What? Ah,. . . where did you see me?

So-hi: . . . Ah.. . do come and see us often.

Sang-bŏm: O.K., I will.

(So-hi goes out, glancing back at the money roll. Sangbŏm and Sang-ch'ŏl take up their glasses and drink their juice.) I forgot! *(He takes out three rolls of bills and gives them to Sang-ch'ŏl.)* This is 30 thousand *wŏn.* . . . Please give this to Mother. She said 30 thousand is needed to

celebrate Father's 61st birthday.

(As Sang-bŏm is about to go into his room, Hyŏn So-hi comes out from stage left.) . . . How's it going, So-hi?

So-hi: Ah, hi!

(Hyŏn So-hi turns again, walks to stage right and returns. She seems to be waiting for Tank. Song-bŏm opens the door of his room and enters. So-hi stalks about, waiting for Tank. Through the keyhole of the imaginary door, Sang-bŏm peeps at So-hi. He is astonished to see her cheeks. Disturbed, he paces to and fro in his room. Then he picks up the phone in the corner and begins to dial.)

Sang-bŏm: . . . Hello, operator? Give me the business office for this building please. Yes, is this the business office? Ah, Hello? This is the business office? I'm calling because I have something to ask you. I say. . . the man who lives in room 28. . . could you repeat that? Right. He's called Tank. This morning I saw him packing and moving out. You say he's moved out completely? Do you know where he's gone? You don't? Then what is his room number? It is vacant? Yes, thanks a lot.

(Sang-bŏm hangs up, hesitates a while, opens the door.)

Excuse me. . . .

So-hi: . . . What?

Sang-bŏm: Are you waiting for Tank?

So-hi: Yes.

Sang-bŏm: This morning. . . that man. . . called someone in the business office of this building. . . . He packed and moved out this morning. They say they don't know where he's gone.

(As soon as So-hi hears this, she appears ready to faint. Sang-bŏm clumsily holds her up.)

Ah. . . see this. . . . Hellow. . . let me see. . . Miss. . . Miss Hyŏn. . . see. . . .

(Sang-bŏm carries her into his room and puts her on the sofa. He is perplexed, doesn't know what to do next.)

So-hi: . . . I say. . . please water. . . water. . . .

Sang-bŏm: Water? Yes.

(Sang-bŏm rushes into the next room. Meanwhile So-hi takes a few pills from her handbag and holds them in her palm. Sang-bŏm brings a cup of water and gives it to her. As soon as she takes the glass from him, she attempts to use the water to wash down the pills. Sang-bŏm dives for her, grapples with her, takes the poison away. The glass falls on the floor. Sang-bŏm stands awkwardly holding her against his chest with one arm.)

Sang-bŏm: Calm. . . calm down please. You shouldn't do that. If you die here, it will affect me too. They might think. . . .

So-hi: He betrayed me!

Sang-bŏm: I say, please calm down.

So-hi: (Disengaging herself from Sang-bŏm) Son of a bitch!

Sang-bŏm: What? I'm sorry.

So-hi: I'm not speaking of you.

Sang-bŏm: I understand.

So-hi: That bastard is the worst swindler in the world! He robbed me! He took my money! Not only mine, but my friend's! He just packed up and took off! He's a common criminal, that's what he is! I'm. . . I'm. . . that's the end! That's it!

(So-hi begins to cry.)

Sang-bŏm: Don't cry. Don't cry.

So-hi: I. . . I must die.

Sang-bŏm: Please not in this room, though. . . .

So-hi: Ah, I'm suffocating. I'm betrayed! Betrayed!

(Sang-bŏm exits stage left and returns with a bottle of wine.)

Sang-bŏm: This is. . . wine. . . which my brother left. . . . I heard wine's the best sedative. Take some. Please.

So-hi: (Accepting the wine) You think I'm no good anyway, I might as well accept your wine. I'm so low that I've ever been betrayed by a hoodlum like Tank. I want to get drunk.

Sang-bŏm: Tank never returned that can of coffee and box of sugar he borrowed from me.

So-hi: You must be as stupid as I am.

Sang-bŏm: Well. . . I used to be. . . long ago. . . but now I've changed my outlook.

(So-hi drinks directly from the bottle as if blowing a trumpet. Frightened by this spectacle, Sang-bŏm sinks slowly onto a chair. Then he stands abruptly, distressed by So-hi's loud choking coughs.)

What can I. . . Miss Hyŏn. . . are you all right?

So-hi: . . . My. . . please slap my back.

Sang-bŏm: Your back?

(Holding So-hi by one arm, Sang-bŏm slaps her back as requested.) Do you feel any better?

So-hi: Brr! It's so stuffy in here! Hold me please, I'm shivering. . . please, not quite so tight.

Sang-bŏm: You mean. . . like this?

So-hi: Yes. . . Oh! I'm sorry. I get cold so easily. Please hold me a little tighter. . . a little more. . . ah, it's all because of that goddamn son of a bitch!

Sang-bŏm: What? Yes. . . .

So-hi: One minute please. . . .

(She takes another long pull at the bottle.)

Sang-bŏm: But. . . if you drink too much, it will hurt you. . . .

So-hi: What difference does it make? I'm ruined already! He's deserted me. . . . I'll get as goddamn drunk as I want. Ah, it's stuffy in here. Men are all the same.

Sang-bŏm: I'm sorry.

So-hi: *(Waving at him)* I don't mean you. Why are you treating me so kindly?

Sang-bŏm: Lately I've learned that one should be very kind to women.

So-hi: I'm trembling. Hold me please.

Sang-bŏm: Yes. . . like this?

So-hi: Right. Like that. Ah! I'm suffocating. Undo me a little bit, please.

Sang-bŏm: You mean, here?

> *(Sang-bŏm's hands move tremblingly up the back of So-hi's dress as the light in the room fades out. Then, with light music, the light comes up again. A bean curd peddler's bell rings. It is morning. Sang-bŏm emerges stage left with his magazines and dumps them in the garbage box. Then he sits on the sofa and reads a newspaper. So-hi brightly carries in a cup of coffee, serves it to Sang-bŏm, kisses him on the cheek, then flies lightly back to the inner room.)*

Sang-bŏm: (To the audience, as he sips his coffee.)

For the first time in my life I'm drinking coffee made by a woman. *(Standing)* I slept with So-hi last night. You have to grab your chances. Instead of offering a seat, you should take the seat. *(Pointing to the garbage box)* Thanks to So-hi, those magazines which I used to enjoy looking at under the blanket have become useless. Those glamorous girls I could see only in photos. . . or fantasies. . . now I've come up with one of my own in just a few minutes. It was a magnificent gesture by Tank, to leave me Hyŏn So-hi in exchange for my coffee and sugar. This room has become a flower bed.

> *(He looks about with great satisfaction.)*

Ah—there's something more. Our company president has gone off to South Asia with an economic delegation. I saw him off at Kimp'o Airport two days ago. Now, there's no one over me. I'm the boss. For the first time in 31 years I'm enjoying my life. I'm a happy man.

> *(So-hi enters from the next room. Holding her hands, Sang-bŏm whispers to her as they walk lightly around room as if dancing.)*

Ah! What a beautiful life! My love! My rose! My dream! My happiness!

> *(So-hi lets Sang-bŏm's hands fall and returns to the inner room, smiling at him.)*

(To the audience) Each day passes so quickly! My income

has gone up and I'm accumulating property.

(He takes out a camera and binoculars from his cabinet.)
I even bought some binoculars. One Saturday we went on a picnic. All the way to Ui-dong.

(So-hi comes out, throwing on a coat, and puts her arm in Sang-bŏm's. They walk slowly to stage front. Sang-bŏm wears sunglasses and carries his camera and binoculars over his shoulder. As the room light fades, stage center lights up and music evocative of birds and a,pastoral landscape is heard.)

So-hi: *(Arm in arm with Sang-bŏm)* I've never had such a pleasant feeling before. Perhaps this is true happiness. Isn't it? My darling?

Sang-bŏm: Well. . . . It's quite nice to be out in the country after so long.

(They look through the binoculars, still arm in arm.)
I can even see a squirrel playing in the chestnut tree. . . my goodness, look at this. . . . It's general manager Pak. . . no. . . Miss Sŏng. . . the president's daughter-in-law, I mean, his secretary. Look, Mr. Pak and Miss Sŏng are sitting out on the terrace on the second floor of the Full Moon Hotel. . . drinking beer. . . now Mr. Pak is putting his arm around Miss Sŏng's waist. . . .

So-hi: They're human beings.

Sang-bŏm: Human beings?

So-hi: Human beings are all the same, aren't they?

Sang-bŏm: The general manager has five kids, though. . . of course, he has a wife too.

So-hi: That's none of your business.

Sang-bŏm: Yes. . . still, it's important to me.

So-hi: Let's go back to the hotel.

Sang-bŏm: You go ahead. I think I'll go to the Full Moon Hotel for a while. I'll be back soon.

So-hi: For what?

Sang-bŏm: I'll be with you soon, don't worry. Let's walk together down to the fork in the road.

(They exit stage left. Then the spotlight focuses on the office. A-mi sits on the sofa reading a book. A moment later the door of the president's office flies open. Sang-bŏm carries out a shotgun and begins cleaning it.)

A-*mi:* You're doing the shotgun again.

Sang-bŏm: The more I clean this beauty, the more I love it. . . . Tell me, any news of the president?

A-*mi:* Yes, he's in Singapore now.

Sang-bŏm: . . . Have you been to Singapore?

A-*mi:* No, I haven't been in that part of the world yet. After staying in America almost two years. . . .

Sang-bŏm: Ah, when you were in America you met your former husband. . . .

A-*mi:* Right.

Sang-bŏm: Ah, I forgot! *(Pulling out a note from his pocket)* This bill puzzles me.

A-*mi:* What bill is that?

Sang-bŏm: The other day. . . let's see, two days before the president left, the day we made the contract for two-inch steel. . . at the Bando Hotel. You said that the amount the president spent with the American at that time. . . including the money to buy the gift. . . . You said the total amount was 123 thousand?

A-*mi:* . . . Yes, it was.

Sang-bŏm: I gave the money to you.

A-*mi:* And then?

Sang-bŏm: But when I checked with the hotel and the shop you visited, I found the total bill came to only 62 thousand. Therefore, the remaining 61 thousand, other than the actual expenses, was paid to you. . . ?

A-*mi:* . . . With that. . . that money. . . I bought the American another gift on behalf of the president.

Sang-bŏm: (Raising his voice) Ah. . . . Is that right! I understand. There was another gift for this lucky American. The total amount you asked for was exactly equal to. . . yes. I wonder how this misunderstanding could have arisen.

(Awkward silence for a while)

I say, our general manager also studied in America?

A-mi: . . .That's what they say.

Sang-bŏm: Since he's 46 now. . . it was a long time ago, wasn't it?

A-mi: . . . What was a long time ago?

Sang-bŏm: I mean, the time when general manager Pak studied in America.

A-mi: Well?

Sang-bŏm: Since you are 27 now. . . .

A-mi: You're not supposed to talk about a woman's age like that.

Sang-bŏm: I don't mean to do that. . . at any rate there is about a 20 year gap in your ages.

A-mi: . . . Well, what of it?

Sang-bŏm: I'm 15 years younger than he is.

(At this moment, the telephone rings. Sang-bŏm talks on the phone while holding the gun in one hand.) Ah, Hello. Pardon? Ah, manager Pak. Yes, this is the business manager. Yes? Yes? That's right, sir. I paid 20 thousand to the Full Moon Hotel in Ui-dong. I got a phone call from the hotel. I don't know who it was that called. So I went there personally, examined the bill, and paid 20 thousand *wŏn*. Yes? I have the receipt. Yes? I reported that sometimes you went to the hotel with your family for a rest. Yes. Next time I'll ask you before paying the bill. Yes. Good-bye, sir.

(A-mi, looking pale, pretends to read a book.) General manager Pak is a real family man. Whenever he has time he seems to take his family to the country for a rest. What! The stove's run out of oil. Should I work in the president's office. . . temporarily. . . should I become the acting president for about five minutes? Ha, ha. . . .

(Sang-bŏm holds the gun and aims it here and there. He points it at A-mi for a moment. She is frightened. Then Sang-bŏm enters the president's office. A-mi stands, picks up the phone and dials.)

A-mi: It's me. I must see you right away. I'll come over there,
okay? Well, the hotel owner's not so good. Yes.

*(A-mi hangs up and paces around the room. Then she
picks up her handbag and opens the door of the president's
office.)* Mr. Kim, I'm going to the dentist. I'll be back
soon.

*(Sang-bŏm steps out from the president's office still holding
the gun.)*

Sang-bŏm: Dentist? Yes, go ahead.

(A-mi exits, looking sullen.)

(To the audience) I caught general manager Pak and secretary Sŏng in the act. They belong to a high class whose
quality is entirely different from mine. But once they are
caught in a scandalous act they fall into confusion, as you
saw. The Full Moon Hotel never demanded that I pay their
bills. I myself went to the hotel and paid them, just so I would
be able to make general manager Pak uneasy now.

Let's see. . . I have to admit I've got a new desire. Though
I've risen to become the youngest business manager in the
history of this company, I want to climb still higher. I can't
be satisfied with this position which I got thanks to toilet
paper, church connections, and slander against Pae Yŏng-min.
Now I'm going to use the big bait of general manager Pak
and Sŏng A-mi to catch that fat goldfish called "success in
life."

If ordinary people like me try to follow the straight and
narrow, they never even get near the threshold of success in
life. That's why I must use the NEW COMMON SENSE.

(Coming out to stage front) I've been so absorbed in
distinguishing myself at work that somehow two months
have passed without my knowing it. While I've been con-
centrating on the company, a horrifying thing has happened at home. One evening when I returned to my nest, my
apartment where my darling was waiting for me. . . .

*(Sang-bŏm steps toward stage front, opens the door of his
room, enters. The room lights up. Hyŏn So-hi and Tank*

are rolling about beneath the large cross on the wall.)

E. . . h? This. . . .

(The two stand up, recovering slowly from their delirium, somewhat drunk. Liquor bottles and glasses roll on the tea table.)

So-hi: Ah. . . you're home.

Tank: Ah. . . it's a long time, brother Kim.

(Tank stands up and thrusts out his hand, but Sang-bŏm immediately begins fixing his tie. Sang-bŏm refuses to shake his hand.)

Sang-bŏm: Get out of here! Now! Goddamn dogs!

So-hi: Take it easy. Have a glass of wine.

(Sang-bŏm, furious, is about to slap So-hi's cheek, but Tank roughly restrains him.)

Tank: You mustn't use violence against a weak woman.

Sang-bŏm: You!. . . You're nothing but a big thief!. . . What are you, anyway?

Tank: Me a thief? Ha! You don't know who the thief is! Who is it that stole my wife while I was gone?

Sang-bŏm: Your wife?

So-hi: Yes. My actual husband's Tank, though of course you're my legal husband.

Sang-bŏm: I'm your legal husband?

(So-hi jumps to her feet and removes an envelope from her handbag, waving a piece of paper she takes from the envelope.)

So-hi: See this? This is a copy of our marriage certificate.

Sang-bŏm: Marriage certificate? When did I register. . .?

So-hi: You were busy, so I did it myself about a week ago.

Sang-bŏm: I never married you.

Tank: The wedding ceremony, that doesn't matter. Once you're registered you're a married couple. That's it. I'm the witness, as a matter of fact.

Sang-bŏm: A foul witness like you?

So-hi: Now I've been caught in the act of committing adultery with my secret lover. This is serious enough for a divorce.

Isn't it? If you want to divorce me, I'm willing to sign the papers. Here are the divorce papers all ready to be signed. *(She takes another envelope from her handbag.)*

Tank: Again I can be the witness.

Sang-bŏm: Humph! Of course I'll divorce you. Registered our marriage without telling me! Huh! Vicious frauds!

So-hi: But. . . there's a condition if you want this divorce.

Sang-bŏm: Condition?

So-hi: Right. I want 500 thousand *wŏn* as consolation money.

Sang-bŏm: You're a damn robber! Prostitute! 500 thousand *wŏn*?

So-hi: There, you see? I have no choice. I'll have to hang around here.

Tank: Ah, ah, take it easy now. You shouldn't be irrational like that. We're all adults, aren't we? 500 thousand *wŏn* isn't that much to you. . . .

Sang-bŏm: I won't give you even five *wŏn*. No, even if I took back the money which I used to feed a dirty prostitute like you all this time, I still wouldn't be satisfied!

So-hi: Humph! If you sleep with a girl like me for a night, you need at least three thousand, don't you? You haven't paid me even a nickle during the last three months. What's more, I'm such a beautiful woman. . . .

Tank: What, beauty like this deserves a little more.

So-hi: He's used a beautiful woman like me as a hot maid, more than three months. . . . And I was confined in the house all alone during the daytime. . . 500 thousand is not enough, I say. You're the business manager, aren't you? You can afford several millions. Such a trivial amount is no problem to you.

Tank: Hey, Mr. Kim! Miss Hyŏn, you know, she gets a little over-excited sometimes. If she talked with the president in this condition, there's no telling what might happen.

So-hi: You're a church-goer? A bachelor? Think about it and give me 500 thousand *wŏn*. I'll give you two days to think it over. If you don't cough it up by then, I'll have to have a little talk with your company president. Do I have some choice stories for him?

Sang-bŏm: (To the audience) What can I do in a case like this? Those gangsters are completely lacking in common sense. I ran out of the building and wandered the streets. But I've no place to go. I have to sleep at the office.

(Sang-bŏm walks across to his office. A man and woman are heard laughing behind the president's door. Sang-bŏm opens the door a crack, peeks in and closes the door instantly, stunned.)

At this time of night, general manager Pak and A-mi are sitting on the couch? Of course they are not sitting quietly. In fact, they are not sitting at all. Can you imagine what must be going on at my apartment? I may be the only poor working man in the world being tormented by two love affairs at once. I can't be tormented like this forever. The New Common Sense tells me I must take certain measures.

(The telephone rings. Sang-bŏm does not answer it. Finally Sŏng A-mi comes out, hair dissheveled, skirt rumpled. She is frightened to see Sang-bŏm.)

Sang-bŏm: (Picking up the phone) Hello? Yes, I'm Kim Sang-bŏm. What do you want, Tank? You son of a bitch! How did you know I was here. . .? What? You think, it's obvious I have no other place to go? And?. . . then. . .? What time. . .? Ten. . .? O.K. I'll be there.

(To A-mi after hanging up) What's the matter with you?

A-mi: (After touching up her skirt and hair). . . Since when are you keeping an eye on us?

Sang-bŏm: I. . . . What do you mean? I have some work in my desk, I came only to finish it up. . . .

A-mi: By yourself?

Sang-bŏm: . . . No. I came with my friend and. . . .

A-mi: With your friend? All right. . . . Where's your friend. . .?

Sang-bŏm: Yes. . . I say. . . I saw you and general manager Pak in the president's office. . . and I had my friend go. . . .

A-mi: Then your friend also saw us. . . is that what you mean? He's a witness?

Sang-bŏm: . . . What you are talking about. . .?

A-mi: Do you know anything about us?

Sang-bŏm: I don't know a thing, of course not. . . that way my friend calling. I'm afraid I must leave. I'm going without saying hello to general manager Pak. Please extend my regards to him.

> *(Sang-bŏm exits. A-mi stands with folded arms as the office light fades. Sang-bŏm brings out a settee from stage left and sits on it stage front.)*

Sang-bŏm: I'm being threatened by those vicious frauds Tank and So-hi. But at the same time I'm threatening general manager Pak and Sŏng A-mi. I'm chased but I'm also in a position to chase. A while ago Tank called and said he wants to meet me at Pagoda Park. He said he has a good way to clean up this messy situation.

> *(Tank comes out with a cigarette between his teeth and sits down next to Sang-bŏm.)*

Tank: Pretty quiet around here.

Sang-bŏm: Let's get down to business. What is it you're proposing?

Tank: I'm telling you, you shouldn't treat a woman like that. You must handle them tenderly.

Sang-bŏm: Goddamn it, I didn't come to listen to a sermon. What's your proposal?

Tank: Since today is the 23rd. . . tomorrow's the 24th. Therefore, that makes it the day before payday, right? Payday is the 25th?

Sang-bŏm: How would you know about paydays? Are you trying to tell me somebody hired you?

Tank: It's just common sense. . . so, tomorrow, the 24th, you'll be preparing to pay salaries to the company workers, because you're business manager. The salaries will be paid at one o'clock in the afternoon of the 25th? So-hi told me this. Therefore, the business manager and the secretary will stay in the office, getting ready to pay the salaries, while everyone else goes out for lunch. I mean, just you and the secretary and 420 million *wŏn*. Right? 420 million *wŏn!* Now that's big money. If I pay a visit to the office at 12:30 or so and threaten you with a gun or ·a bomb, you'll have to turn the 420 million over to me. Get it? As a mere business manager you won't have any choice but to go along with it. They'll go for the story, no worry about that. And in return I'll be very generous with you. I'll make sure So-hi never shows her face in your place again.

Sang-bŏm: So-hi?

Tank: Do you think you can save yourself from So-hi with a mere 50 million *wŏn?* She'll be bugging you the rest of your life. This won't be the last time! If you tried to get 50 million *wŏn,* you'd have to do something risky, some complicated financial hankypanky. Too risky! You'd better be robbed of 420 million of the company's money than have to commit some crime yourself, wouldn't you? I think so. I can guarantee you that you'll never see So-hi again.

   (Tank stands up and tosses away his cigarette butt.) Then. . . I'll see you at 12:25 on the 25th at your office. You won't forget. I know you won't forget.

Sang-bŏm: Then. . . you'll return the marriage certificate and the divorce papers to me?

Tank: . . . After I get the 420 million. At your office—I'll see you at 12:25 on the 25th. After that, you won't have to put up any more with Hyŏn So-hi you can be sure of that. If anything does happen just say you don't know anything about it. ·

   (Tank strolls away. The office lights up and A-mi is seen counting piles of money. Sang-bŏm comes of the president's office carrying an approved document.)

Sang-bŏm: You're working too hard.

*(Without any reply A-mi continues to count out stacks
of bills and put them into envelopes. Sang-bŏm glares
impatiently at his watch. The president comes out.
Sang-bŏm stands and bows to him.)*

President: Will the salaries be ready on time?

Sang-bŏm: Yes, sir! At one o'clock on the dot, no problem, sir.

President: I'll be at the Hongpa restaurant right across the
street. I'm having lunch with Dr. Pak. . . .

Sang-bŏm: Yes, sir. If anything comes up, I'll let you know, sir.

    (The president exits. Sang-bŏm restlessly paces the stage.)

Say. . . . Are you going to have some lunch, Miss Sŏng?

A-mi: Am I in any condition to eat?

Sang-bŏm: I'll take care of this. Why don't you go have lunch
with the president?

A-mi: If you tried to take care of all this by yourself, the pay
would never be ready on time.

Sang-bŏm: . . .The time is now. . . *(He looks at his watch.)*
according to my watch it's 12:25. . . . I say. . . . What time
do you have?

A-mi: (Glancing at her watch, annoyed) It's exactly twenty-
five minutes after twelve.

*Sang-bŏm: (Again sitting behind his desk, face to face with
her)* Exactly twelve-twenty-five. . . .

    *(Tank comes on stage wearing a derby pulled low over
his eyes. He carries a suitcase. A-mi stops her work to
watch Tank.)*

A-mi: Pardon me. . . may I ask whom you're looking for. . .?

    *(Instead of answering Tank thrusts a revolver at her.
A-mi is so stunned she stands up. Then she faints.)*

Tank: Anybody in there. . .?

    (Sang-bŏm shakes his head.) Now, put all this in my
bag. Pronto!

Sang-bŏm: Humph! You arrived exactly on time!

Tank: Gentlemen should always be on time.

    (Sang-bŏm is placing the stacks of bills in the bag.)

Sang-bŏm: Since you say you're a gentleman, just be sure

you keep your promise.

Tank: What promise?

Sang-bŏm: The marriage certificate. The divorce papers.

Tank: (Taking out an envelope and showing it to him) You mean these? You'll get these when I get the money, just as we promised. It's like a business contract, you might say.

(Sang-bŏm finishes putting the money in the suitcase, closes it, thrusts it at Tank.)

Sang-bŏm: Now, let's close the deal.

(They exchange the suitcase and the envelope.)

Tank: I'm. . . I'm not staying in Korea. You'll be glad to hear that. Ah, and. . . I have another promise to keep. . . .

(Taking out a woman's stocking from his inner pocket) Keep this too as a souvenir.

Sang-bŏm: You murdered So-hi. . .?

Tank: I told you, I keep my word.

Sang-bŏm: You strangled her with this. . .?

Tank: Tsk, Tsk! How can you talk like that? Perhaps she's having lunch in heaven by now. Good work, Sang-bŏm!

(Tank exist leisurely, carrying the suitcase. Sang-bŏm meditates intensely for an instant, clutching the envelope and the stocking. Then he thrusts the envelope into his inner pocket, the stocking into his rear trouser pocket. He pulls out the shotgun from beneath his desk and rushes out. A short time later two shotgun blasts are heard. Sang-bŏm returns carrying the shotgun. He kneels beside A-mi, who remains in a deep faint, and gently lifts the upper part of her body and embraces her. He gradually tightens the embrace. Then the president rushes in and is startled at the sight of A-mi and Sang-bŏm.)

President: My God! Is anybody wounded?

(Sang-bŏm arranges A-mi's body on the floor and gently shakes her. After a moment she opens her eyes and looks around.)

Sang-bŏm: You were stunned. Everything's all right now.
I grabbed him.

A-mi: The robber. . .?

President: (Grasping Sang-bŏm's hand) You're a good boy!
You did an excellent job! My thanks to you! People came
running out from building yelling that a robber had
broken into our company and. . . I was so frightened. . . .
Ah, you're brave, very brave! God helped you! Yes, I
believe God helped you.

Sang-bŏm: Is that guy dead?

President: Dead, dead! Ah, good work, good work!
*(A-mi picks herself up and is about to exist. Sang-bŏm
runs to stop her.)*

A-mi: What happened to the thief, the thief. . .?

President: We got him. With God's help.

A-mi: Who got him?

President: Manager Kim over there, he did it.

A-mi: (Shaking her head as if it's hard to believe) Let me. . .
go to the restroom.
*(Again she shakes her head. Holding the shotgun with
one hand, Sang-bŏm throws the other around her waist.
When the president sees this, he nods approvingly. At
last A-mi pushes Sang-bŏm away and goes out.)*

Sang-bŏm: Sir, I'm very sorry I was unable to prevent this
robbery.

President: Not at all! I say, it's supernatural. Now, let's
hurry, we must report it to the police.
(Accepting the shotgun from Sang-bŏm) Heroic, this
was an heroic action. . . . By the way. . . since when. . .
have you had such a relationship with secretary Sŏng?

Sang-bŏm: Ah. . . well, I don't know what to say. . . it
happened naturally.

President: You love Miss Sŏng, then?

Sang-bŏm: Why, of course. . . .

President: Of course secretary Sŏng also loves you. . . .

Sang-bŏm: Well. . . .

President: I know! I know! I can understand it. You have
integrity. I can't go on forever insisting that she's my
daughter-in-law. Perhaps my son in his grave would
rather see her marry again, I could understand that. . . .
At any rate you did an excellent job for the company.

Sang-bŏm: (Stepping toward the audience) Things have
worked out so well that I feel rather dizzy. The next day
the president gathered everyone in the company and
praised me before them. After that he gave me a reward
of 50 million *wŏn*, because I saved the company 420
million *wŏn*. What's more, I've been specially promoted
to managing director. I've become a hero at the company and for all Seoul citizens. As a result, business is
picking up at the company. Orders are flooding in from
all over the place.

What it amounts to is this. Tank lost. He lost because
he made the mistake of telling me he had murdered Hyŏn
So-hi. His plan fell apart at that moment. As soon as
I realized that Tank had killed her, my New Common
Sense went into operation. Two people were killed, it's
true, but I don't feel even a trifle uneasy.

You think this is curious? Well. . . isn't it true that I
shot him in my own self-defense, quite legitimately?
That's how I see it. Certainly I prefer to believe that's
the correct interpretation.

A few days later, I called Sŏng A-mi to my hotel. Since
I'd caught the poor doll in *flagrante delicto*, she had no
choice but to show up without protest at my room.

*(Sŏng A-mi enters stage left, walks up through stage
front to the door of the room. She stands there, obviously
angry. A few moments later, she knocks on the door as
if she has no choice.)*

Sang-bŏm: (Standing up) Come in.

*(Although she has opened the door, she still stands at
the threshold.)* Come in, please!

(A-mi steps in without a word, stands.) Have a seat

over here, please!

A-mi: I'm all right just like this. Now what is it you want?
I've no time to waste.

Sang-bŏm: But, please, I'd like you to sit down. . . .

A-mi: In five minutes I'm going to leave.

(A-mi sits down.)

Sang-bŏm: What's your hurry? Is general manager Pak
waiting outside?

(A-mi doesn't reply.) Would you like some coffee?

A-mi: Please, let's get on with it. What is it that's so important?

Sang-bŏm: I'll tell you, don't worry.

A-mi: Go ahead. Nowadays manager Kim, you are. . . .

Sang-bŏm: Ah, I'm managing director.

A-mi: Nowadays you're in seventh heaven, aren't you? All
the newspapers write about you and you've risen so high
for someone so young. . . you were given a reward of
50 million *wŏn*. . . .

Sang-bŏm: Thank you for the compliments. I'm going to get
a good shotgun with that money.

A-mi: I wonder if you could speak to me about the important thing now.

Sang-bŏm: O.K., I will. You're an intelligent woman edu-
cated in America.

A-mi: And?

Sang-bŏm: What's more you're very beautiful.

A-mi: Thank you.

Sang-bŏm: Above all, you're a smart woman.

A-mi: Oh my! What on earth, this man. . . .

Sang-bŏm: Just a moment. And you're passionately in love
with general manager Pak. In fact, you're deeply involved
with a man who has not only a wife but several kids as
well. I saw the two of you sleeping together at a hotel.

A-mi: That's not true!

Sang-bŏm: Then, may I show you a photograph I took? I
have many other photos and some reports from a detec-
tive agency. You began to flirt around less than six months

after your husband's death. Even if I mysteriously vanished, by the way, there's another person, a friend of mine, who will testify about your scandalous relations with general manager Pak. So you can stop thinking about getting rid of me, it won't work. . . . And there's something else I want to talk with you about—all the company money that's gone into your purse. That money belongs to your father-in-law, so you think you can be reckless with it. Without telling him, of course. One might say you've stolen that money.

A-mi: I know what you want. Tell me, manager Kim. . . . No, managing director Kim. . . exactly how much do you want? Let's get down to specifics. How much *wŏn?*

Sang-bŏm: Well. . . your late husband. . . let's see, a few days before the president's son died, he changed his will and left all his property entirely to his father's care.

A-mi: (Flying into a rage) How did you find out about that?

Sang-bŏm: A number of times I've visited the president's lawyer on company business. . . . What's more, I know something even more important. In the event of your remarriage, the president is to return the property to you. That is, if he thinks your new husband is a man of ability. and character. Your late husband was a more generous man than Christ himself.

A-mi: He was a different kind of man from a vicious fraud like you!

Sang-bŏm: I'd say he was much too good a man for an adulteress like you.

A-mi: Oh, for God's sake! You brought me here, now what are you going to do with me?

Sang-bŏm: I want to marry you. •

A-mi: Oh, my God. . . . What?

Sang-bŏm: I said, I want to marry Miss Sŏng A-mi.

A-mi: Marry a man like you. . .? Incredible!

Sang-bŏm: Incredible? Not at all. . . why, when we're married. . . I'll become just as generous to you as your Christ-like husband. I'll take care of feeding the other five in your family and I'll put your brother and sister through college. Our fortunes will go up and up. . . . When the president retires, you'll be the new president's wife. . . .

A-mi: Oh, my God.

Sang-bŏm: It's obvious I'll become the new president, isn't it? At any rate, the president will approve of your marrying me.

A-mi: If I refuse, then what do you intend to do?

Sang-bŏm: Refuse? A beautiful, smart woman like you refuse such a wonderful offer? That would be a real mistake. You know, I also sometimes desire to sleep with you. You're very beautiful and. . . .

A-mi: I can't stand it!

(A-mi jumps to her feet and flies furiously toward the door.)

Sang-bŏm: Think it over! It's just an offer. If you don't like it, go home, fine. . . . If you accept it, come back here and sit down again. . . .

(A-mi hesitates for a while and sits on the chair again. The room light slowly fades out as Sang-bŏm steps stage front and addresses the audience.) And that's how it happened that I slept with Sŏng A-mi that night. It was so different from the first night in bed with Hyŏn So-hi. I couldn't feel any emotion or excitement at all.

All that was left was only a fearfully strong sense of conquest and victory.

After a certain period A-mi and I had our wedding ceremony on a snowy day. We invited a few close friends and relatives.

(The president, Sang-hak, Pae Yŏng-min, Mrs. Mun, Yong-ja, and A-mi come out carrying drinks, talking cheerily.)

Humph! We invited general manager Pak too. But he tells us he's not feeling well—a bad case of diarrhea hit him early this morning.

President: Now, did you say when your plane leaves?

Sang-bŏm: 2:30, sir.

President: You'd better hurry up. Don't forget, the mountain behind the hotel is a good place for hunting deer. I'm afraid you'll stay in your suite just because this trip is a honeymoon. I'm reminding you, don't forget to go hunting. Bring me back a few deer or rabbits. *(To Pae Yŏng-min)* Manager Pae, the gift. . . .

　　(Yŏng-min exits.) I have a special gift for you.

Sang-bŏm: You've already given me so many presents. . . .

　　(Pae Yŏng-min brings out a shotgun.)

Pae Yŏng-min: Managing director Kim, sir! Congratulations. Ha, ha. . . .

President: I say, this, this! This is a two chamber-revolver made in Belgium. That's right! This is the best possible honeymoon gift. With this gift you can protect your wife and. . . go hunting. . . .

Sang-bŏm: Thank you, sir.

　　(As Sang-bŏm accepts the gun, Sang-ch'ŏl runs on stage.)

Sang-ch'ŏl: Brother! Brother!

Sang-bŏm: You're here!

Sang-ch'ŏl: I'm sorry I'm late. But I did it! I did it!

Sang-hak: What? Ah, you passed the exam?

Sang-ch'ŏl: Right. I passed! I passed!

President: Now I say, everyone, the time's getting short. We'd better be going. We'll be outside, Sang-bŏm. I'm sure these three brothers would like to have a word in private before we go. . . .

　　(All of them extt, leaving the three brothers.)

A-mi: Then. . . .

　　(A-mi also exits.)

Sang-bŏm: *(To Sang-ch'ŏl)* Great work!

Sang-ch'ŏl: It took three years. Three years!

Sang-hak: However long it took, I'm very happy for you. . . .

　　I've passed too, by the way.

Sang-bŏm: You too, brother?

Sang-hak: I've. . . given up my professorship!

Sang-bŏm: When?

Sang-hak: Ever since my marriage, I've lived only to take care of my family. When I was working at the college, I found I couldn't make enough to feed my family. Especially not if I tried to pursue my rocket research. Therefore, I became a primary school teacher.

Sang-ch'ŏl: You mean. . . a primary school teacher?

Sang-hak: Actually it's a private primary school. It pays me twice what the college did. What a world! A primary school teacher makes more than a college professor! The only reason I could do this is that I graduated from a teacher's college in the old days. The principal at the primary school happens to be a friend of mine. I thought this was important if I was to have a suitable position. Nowadays I rather feel free.

Sang-ch'ŏl: Can you make any money on the side?

Sang-hak: Well, look, it's getting late. We'd better be going.

Sang-ch'ŏl: Father refused to come, you know. Because brother didn't marry a virgin.

Sang-bŏm: (To the audience as soon as Sang-hak and Sang-ch'ŏl exeunt) My brother Sang-ch'ŏl finally became a trainee working at the bottom of an administrative section. After three years of blood and sweat! With great difficulty he managed to squeeze through the gate into the world of common sense. Of course, his future remains rather. . . vague. And yet he himself seems very satisfied, at least at the moment.

On the other hand, my other brother demoted himself to a primary school teacher. Yet he too seems to feel happy in his improved ability to take care of his family. And what about me? I've become a bigwig of a steel company; I'm no longer bothered by things like money and status. In the future. . . well. . . what awaits me?

(A-mi brings out two chairs and puts them side by side at stage front. Sang-bŏm and A-mi sit on the chairs. The

thundering sound of an airplane is heard.)

Here we are, a newly married couple, and we have nothing to say to each other. Our plane is flying to Kangwŏn Province, but we have the feeling we're flying into endless empty space; we feel it stretching ahead forever. Shortly before the plane landed, A-mi opened her mouth for the first time.

A-mi: Darling. . . excuse me. . . .

Sang-bŏm: You don't look too well. . . are you feeling all right?

A-mi: No. . . I'm afraid I'm. . . . I'm pregnant.

Sang-bŏm: Pregnant? You don't mean. . . a baby?

A-mi: Yes.

Sang-bŏm: . . . You'd better take good care of yourself.

A-mi: We've arrived.

(A-mi unfastens an imaginary seatbelt. Sang-bŏm sits vacantly without moving.)

Sang-bŏm: My mind was disturbed by this. She told me there's new life in her belly. Even in the hotel I couldn't find any peace of mind.

(A-mi stands up and exits.)

A new life growing in A-mi's belly! As for my part in it . . . it couldn't possibly be my baby. At any rate, whomever it belongs to, it will be born as my baby as far as the law's concerned. When that tiny boy or girl that's not my own arrives in the world with the usual tears and shrieks, what will my reaction be? A puppy begotten by a wolf and a fox. I'll have to believe a wolf is the same as a dog. I'll have to believe it's a puppy which will grow up to be very much like me. While the true parents, that male wolf and that female fox, are grinning at us from a distance, we'll have to be happy with telling each other we're alike. . . .

I sat on this chair, but it was so painful that I moved to the other one. *(He moves to other chair.)* I was blown here by the wind of a New Common Sense, you might say. . . . But I discovered that in the end they're both the same: the only difference is the location. Uneasiness and anxiety still follow me just as before. Right now I can see the image of my brother Sang-ch'ŏl, who is doing something. . . sweating heavily. . . excited. The face of my other brother smiling and singing with his children—that too comes into my mind. Still. . . they don't know this society. . . . Or is it because they know it very well that they've chosen their particular paths?

The next evening Pae Yŏng-min, who was assigned to this remote area, came to visit me.

(Pae Yŏng-min enters with an armful of flowers.)

Pae Yŏng-min: How are you, sir? I'm sorry to visit you at night like this. . . . Where is Mrs. Kim?

Sang-bŏm: She's in the bathroom. Are those flowers for me or my lovely wife?

Pae Yŏng-min: These? They're for both of you, of course. . . . By the way. . . how's this hotel? Is it quiet? *(No reaction from Sang-bŏm)* The atmosphere is pretty romantic. . . .

Sang-bŏm: It's sentimental.

Pae Yŏng-min: That's the perfect word. The atmosphere is pretty sentimental.

Sang-bŏm: No, it's comical.

Pae Yŏng-min: . . . That's right. It's comical, sir!

Sang-bŏm: Well. . . a still better word is 'tragic'!

Pae Yŏng-min: What, sir? Tragic. . .?

Sang-bŏm: From a larger perspective I'd say 'comical' is actually the best description.

Pae Yŏng-min: . . . Ah, a comical atmosphere! That's an excellent way to put it. It's a very literary expression. Since I've been living in this isolated area, I haven't been able to read as many books as I'd like. . . . I've always loved literature, though. . . since I came to these mountains, I haven't been able to read much. . . .

Sang-bŏm: I'd think a quiet area like this would be very good for reading. . . .

Pae Yŏng-min: Temperamentally. . . and because of my

family situation. . . any way one looks at it, in fact, to be assigned to Seoul would be. . . .

Sang-bŏm: Well! In this dusty corner graft would be very difficult.

Pae Yŏng-min: What, sir? Graft? I don't know what you're talking about, sir. . . .

(At this moment A-mi comes out of the bathroom wearing only a negligee. Yŏng-min is embarrassed.)

I brought these flowers for you. . . .

(He hesitates and hands them to Sang-bŏm.) I'll wait in the tearoom downstairs. Mrs. Kim, congratulations.

(Pae Yŏng-min exits.)

A-mi: When did he drop in? And what is he congratulating me on?

Sang-bŏm: Well. . . perhaps on the baby in your belly.

A-mi: Humph! You've got this baby on the brain!

Sang-bŏm: Because it's a love baby!. . . You look very good in that nightgown. It's almost like wearing nothing at all.

A-mi: Thank you.

Sang-bŏm: How strange it is. . . .

A-mi: What are you getting at?

Sang-bŏm: Well, I'd say women look even more beautiful without clothes than with them.

A-mi: . . . You've made a great discovery.

(At this time the telephone rings noisily.) Answer the phone, please.

Sang-bŏm: I think it must be our Mr. Pae, who's dreaming of the streets of Seoul in the tearoom downstairs. *(Sang-bŏm picks up the phone.)* Hello? Yes? Long distance from Seoul? Who? Sŏng A-mi? Just a moment. It's long distance from Seoul. *(He gives the phone to A-mi.)*

A-mi: Hello? Yes? Go ahead, please. . . ah. . . . *(She glances at Sang-bŏm.)* Yes, I'm fine. How's it with you?. . . Don't worry. . . . Is it cold even in Seoul now?. . . Yes. . . I'm O.K. I have no choice but to endure. . . . Yes. . . I'll see you when I get to Seoul. Bye bye.

(She reluctantly hangs up.)

. . . It was my mother.

Sang-bŏm: Ah, it was your mother. . . . By any chance, did she inquire about her new son-in-law? She's a very energetic woman! To make a long distance call at her age. . . even you had to shout into the phone. . . . Why didn't you talk a little longer?. . . We don't have to worry about the cost.

A-mi: I'll be out after I change.

(A-mi enters her room silently. Sang-bŏm sits on the chair without moving. Pae Yŏng-min comes in again.)

Pae Yŏng-min: *(Thrusting a note into his hand)* Sir, forgive my forgetfulness. There's a telegram for you from company headquarters in Seoul. I forgot about it.

Sang-bŏm: What does it say. . .?

Pae Yŏng-min: It says you should be in Pusan by 5 o'clock tomorrow evening.

Sang-bŏm: In Pusan?

Pae Yŏng-min At the Tongnae Hotel. The president isn't feeling well. . . . He wants you to take his place in Pusan and sign the contract concerning construction of the plant . . . our third plant, sir!

Sang-bŏm: My honeymoon is supposed to last a full week. . . .

Pae Yŏng-min: There's no reason you couldn't continue enjoying your honeymoon in Pusan, is there sir?

Sang-bŏm: Let's go down to the tearoom. The drinks are on me.

Pae Yŏng-min: Are you a drinking man, sir?

Sang-bŏm: I'm about to be from now on. And while we're drinking, let's talk about this matter of transferring you to Seoul.

Pae Yŏng-min: Thank you, sir.

Sang-bŏm: All I can do now is. . . drink. . . then. . . you go ahead.

(Pae Yŏng-min exits first.)

Hello! My darling!. . . My A-mi! A-mi!

(Sang-bŏm is almost screaming. Sŏng A-mi, frightened, runs on stage, still slipping on her clothes.)

A-mi: What's going on? Why are you shouting my name like that?

Sang-bŏm: Because I want to see you. Well. . . are you happy?

A-mi: (Sarcastically) Happy?

Sang-bŏm: Humph! I'm supposed to go to Pusan tomorrow. The president ordered me to. Manager Pae received a telegram. He wants me to go down as soon as possible. Well, what about you. . . you want to go?

A-mi: Me?. . . well. . . I feel so heavy. . . .

Sang-bŏm: Then you'll go on up to Seoul?

A-mi: I think it's better. How long will you stay in Pusan?

Sang-bŏm: Well, how long do you want me to stay in Pusan?

A-mi: How should I know. . .?

Sang-bŏm: I'll call you from Pusan. You're pretty.

A-mi: Don't be foolish.

Sang-bŏm: (Holding A-mi in his arms) When is our baby. . .?

A-mi: It's due in August next year.

Sang-bŏm: (Gently shaking A-mi) Our baby! It'll be very pretty! It's our love baby. I'm happy! Happy! I have money, a high position and a beautiful wife. And now a baby's on the way!

A-mi: Humph! Oh, my! You, tears. . . . You're a man. . . . Why the tears?

Sang-bŏm: Because I'm too happy! I'm so happy that I'm crying. Well, I think I'll go downstairs and get a drink. Will you come with me?

A-mi: I feel so heavy. . . .

Sang-bŏm: Yes, you must rest. Starting today, I'm learning how to be a drinking man. . . . You'd better make a long distance call to Seoul.

A-mi: What are you talking about?

Sang-bŏm: Ah, since our honeymoon plans have been changed, you should call. You have to go up to Seoul, so call someone and tell him to get our nest in good shape.

A-mi: All right, I will.

> *(Sang-bŏm exits. A moment later A-mi picks up the phone.)* Hello, operator? This is a long distance call, person to person. The number is Seoul 70-3838. I want to speak with Mr. Pak Ho-p'il. Please ring me as soon as you get through.

> *(The room lights fade as she hangs up. Then a spotlight focuses on Sang-bŏm, who is sitting on a chair stage front. He holds his shotgun in his hands. A train-whistle sounds; then the sound of a fierce blizzard.)*

Sang-bŏm: I've changed trains several times and now I'm on the last leg of the trip to Pusan. Outside the window there's a roaring snowstorm; all I can see is white. I drank too much last night. I'm so badly hung over I feel as if my brains are about to burst out of my head. . . . This shotgun! I don't know why, but I feel very uneasy about it. Perhaps that's why I'm holding it like this.

My wife A-mi left for Seoul. I've got a job to do. . . it's such a trifling thing. What's the use thinking about it? Sŏng A-mi. . . it's just possible that the baby in my bride's belly is my own. I must consciously force myself to think that this baby which will be born next August is truly my own. No. . . .

> *(He takes a coin from his pocket and flips it.)*

Ha, ha. It's heads: It might be my own baby. I'll try to believe that. Do I have any choice? I can try to believe. . . .

> *(The snowstorm roars at an ever-higher pitch; the whistle shrieks itself hoarse as if the train is going at its maximum speed, or beyond, and the curtain falls slowly.)*

The Drug Peddler

by O T'ae-sŏk
translated by Sŏl Sun-bong

A drug peddler enters with his wife who plays the role of singer in his one-man act. He starts to hang strips of paper with names of drugs written on them onto a clothesline with clothespins, while putting on a talkshow. The subjects of his talk are random and as wide-ranged as they are fast-shifting. He begins by talking about the general topics of the times, or about the weather. But in a moment his harangue turns to a ridiculing tirade at the expense of his wife who appears to be rather dumb, or he starts lamenting his bad fortune. Sometimes he attacks a member of the audience who happens to come in late and continues his harangue at his expense by making fun of him.

The wife who is a drummer as well as a singer comes in from time to time with her singing and drumming as the turn of the act calls for them. There is no set rule as to when she should come in. She sings or drums when there is a pause in her husband's act appropriate for her part but otherwise stays behind.

(After preliminary drumming, noise-making, and talking by way of warming-up)

This is a story of a long long long time ago. It was when the trams were being put out of business. This was when I was honorably dismissed from my job and as a result stopped collecting the tickets at a tramcar. I started thinking: What should I do with the hundred thousand *wŏn* I receive as retirement money?

I rode to the suburbs of Seoul and took a tour of the Pavilion of Eight Angles to calm my mind and think up a solution for my problem. But it was no use. Finally, or I should say by luck, I paid a visit to the zoo at Ch'anggyŏng Palace for any clue the place might have for me, and lo, who did I find there but an old pal of mine from my old village, with a camera hanging from his shoulder and an arm-band on his arm saying: Special Member. Now what would this mean, do you people know?

What the two words meant was that the person who had that arm-band around his arm was entitled to make money at the zoo every day. You must forget the time making money, I said. Just get a camera and I will get you the band, he said. Thus bagan my new life, a life of pressing the shutter. That is, I became one of the Special Members of the zoo. But my problem still remained unsolved, you see. Because things turned out to be pretty much different from what I'd figured them to be. The crux of the matter was that the Special Members whom I had figured to be no more than four, five, or seven, eight, turned out to be forty-two. Therefore, I did not forget the time because there was so much money to make but because there was a lot of competition pressing the shutter. I know you wouldn't be surprised, because after all it was a competition of one against forty-two! And what could one do with this situation? Could he eat up the whole lot or drink them down, I ask you? I could, of course, do neither, as you wise folks may have guessed.

So I sat by the lake in the zoo for a whole seven days and thought, nearly wrecking my brains with thinking. But then one day, as I sat by the water as usual, a sheat-fish as big as half of a human arm with whiskers three feet long leaped out of the water, and flapping his tail he made this sound, *(mimicking a horse neighing)* you see, like when a he-horse neighs to a she-horse.

I said to myself, what is this, I never heard of a sheat-fish neighing like a horse?

Aha, I said, it must be that, at the moment this one leaped out of the water, there happened to pass a horse, in Wŏnnamdong Street, right next to the wall of the zoo, who saw something which aroused him improperly. But then, just as I said this to myself, I saw another squirt of water rising in front of my eyes and in it found another sheat-fish. This one produced the sound of a roaring tiger. But again I said, it must be that one of the tigers of the zoo happened to roar at the same time as this fish leaped up. But again, another sheat-fish jumped out of the water and this time made the sound of a rooster crowing. He crowed again and again. *(Shaking his head)* Let's see now, I said and began thinking. O, yes, that's it.

The twelve-animal zodiacal system did not apply to humans only. It applied to the fish, as well, I found out. So, the first sheat-fish that made the sound of a horse was born under the sign of a horse. Likewise, the second one that made the sound of a tiger was born under the sign of a tiger and the third under that of a rooster. The strange sight I witnessed, therefore, was just a show-off of their birth signs on the part of those fish.

No! Yes! It was just as I thought. I found this out after I took pictures of the fish next day and looked at the developed pictures. The one that made the sound of a mouse turned out, in the picture, to look like a mouse with black beady eyes, and the one that made the sound of a rooster looked very much like a rooster. And of course the one that came out and made the sound of a sheep had the look of a sheep. Now what can this

display of physiognomy mean, I wondered. That's it. It must
be the Dragon King who lives in the deep water sending up his
messengers to me. It could be that he was charmed by my
appearance and wants to wed his daughter to me. But what is
the message these creatures are trying to give me?

(Clapping his knee excitedly) That's it, that's it, that's it.

What is your zodiacal sign, Ma'am? Did you say monkey? In
that case, shall we walk over to that corner? May I take a picture of you, right here, in company of your life's companion?
Where else would you have the opportunity to have a picture
taken with the one who has the very identity of your zodiac?
This is the only place you can do that, don't you agree,
Ma'am? I was born in the year of the rooster. Is that so, cock-a-
doodle-doo. Aha, so your zodiac is horse, is it? If you will walk
over to that corner with me, you will find the small-size horses
from Cheju Island. Or is it snake? Mouse? Rooster? No? O, I
see, it must be tiger. Yes, it must be so. Then, sir, would you
please move over in this direction with me? One of the tigers
came from China and the other came from India. Another
came from across the demilitarized zone and the last one is
from across something called the unification zone or some such
thing, I forget what. Now, as life's companion, could anyone
find an animal more handsome and powerful than a tiger?
Impossible! I could take a picture of you so it would look as if
you were riding a tiger. It's simple. You see the rail in front of
the cage? You just step on it and sort of crouch, like when you
are sitting over your toilet pit. You only need to bend your
knees a little, like this, and I will take care of the rest. No
problem. It's all a matter of choosing the right angle. When
you go home, you can tell your daughter-in-law and grandson
how you travelled by the night on the back of a tiger, and
show the picture, the regulation name-card size, too!

Or you could have it taken so it would look as if you were
carrying it on one shoulder. Now, wouldn't it be something!
When you stand up with that animal there which weighs more
than four oxen hanging from your shoulder, even the thousand-

li long Nakdong River will look shorter than this line on my palm. So, now, click.

And you, Grandma?

Did you say mouse? Ah, then I will guide you to the white mouse. He is as white as white jade and fine hemp of Hansan. He is a Russian mouse called marmot. That? No, that's the polar bear. No, it's not white because it's old. It's only three years old. Came from Alaska. Yes, yes, Grandma, it's bear, not a mouse. If your grandchildren ask you what it is, don't tell them it's big mouse. Polar bear, ramie bear, we'll raise them up high, ahoy, so they'll shine afar. Click.

Cock-a-doodle-doo, year of the rooster, is it? No, just follow me. That won't do. That's just an ordinary chicken that you find in your yard, at the house of the barbequed-chicken, and at that House of Willows where they serve you pot-boiled chicken. Come, come, come with me. There's this crow-bone-chicken, ahem, with shiny black feathers like virgin's hair. Wouldn't you like to be his companion for life, click!

Year of the ox? Horse? Dog? What? You were born in year of the elephant? You're joking. But, why not, heh, heh, we could use another zodiac. We could even make one with the thing that's made with the leech eaten by that which is white on the outside but black on the inside heron. (From an old poem which admonished the heron not to laugh at the crow because it looks black.) Click. What? What of it? Why can't I take a picture with my mouth when a person is allowed to adopt the elephant as his zodiac?

Year of the dog? No, that's the otter, not the dog. But you might say it's a kind of dog since we call it 'water dog,' also. Click, click, click, click, click.

It was phenomenal. I ran by myself, far ahead of the others. I took more orders by myself than the sum of orders taken by all 42 of my colleagues together. It was a big time for me. I had nothing to envy the red pepper merchants for.[1] Click, click, click.

However. . . .

(A pause)

It was the season of cherry blossoms when the place was open until ten o'clock at night. I made money everyday. It looked as if I would sweep up all the money there was. But one day toward the end of the season, something happened. Somehow, so many of my customers were chicken folks that day. As soon as I was called to take a picture by a party with a zodiac other than chicken, I would be dragged back to the chicken (that is, crow-bone-chicken) corner to take more pictures of chicken people. But then I remembered that a rooster has the power of chasing evil spirits. So, it looks like the end is going to be even more splendid than before, I thought to myself and clicked. Click, click.

(A pause)

Since the zoo was open until ten o'clock for the cherry blossom festival I had to use so many flashes, the size of a horse's eye and as noisy as firecrackers. And every time the flash went off, the crow-bone-chicken, who is black to the core of its bone and black like the film in the click box, started and blinked as if to find its sight after each explosion of the flash. But the line of chicken people waiting for the picture did not get any shorter and so click click click the camera went on and on and flash flash flash went the firecrackers. In the meantime, the bird's eyeballs were getting blackened like the waning moon and finally as the clicking and the flashing continued its eyes were covered by cataracts and went blind completely.

(He stands with his eyes closed for a moment.)

That night the crow-bone-chicken became a blind bird and I became like this. I mean I can't see right. Everything has become blurred for me. I am not sure whether it's something covering the edges of my eyes or the edges of the objects I see. Anyway there's always this blurry thing around everything I look at. It never budges. It's always there. I can never tell whether it's a clock, a matchbox, an ash tray or a cigarette pack that's lying there.

(He nods once.)

That is, now I have come to live in a world in which an ash tray, matchbox and cigarette case look all the same. Accordingly, Yŏngja, Mija, and Sukja (common names for girls) have become the same and *mijangwŏn* (beauty salon), Yit'aewŏn, and Sariwŏn (both place names) have become one. Likewise, *k'alkuksu* (noodles cut with a knife), *k'altubu* (bean curdle cut in slices with a knife), and *k'almoch'in* are all one to me. In short, I have lost the power of discrimination altogether and I've become a man for whom everything is the same. My regrets were endless. From then on, tears well up in my eyes when I hear a rooster crow.

I should have stuck to the thieving I was trained in. Instead, I let myself foolishly be taken in by a couple of sheat-fish. I should have known better. I should have realized that the world is too clever for me to take in by merely clicking with my finger tip. Did I think it was all that easy? How about a photo? Have a photo taken with your zodiacal companion? Your zodiac is tiger? Sheep? Duck? I only wanted to get the better of the world by using my wits. But was it even wits, I mean the cheap trick I played? In any case, am I to cry over a failure and do nothing? No! I should get hold of a wife before I go completely blind. I need somebody to lead me by the hand if I am to make a living, either as a messager or as a fortune-teller. So I advertised: Looking for a woman who would lead me by the hand. And, believe it or not, my standards were high enough.

(Making a gesture with his body)

Requirements: wise-mother-good-wife type. Doesn't have to be pretty but ordinary good looks and a good figure preferred. If she is patient, obedient, and creative, so much better. And if she is a woman with no defect in intelligence, appearance and character, so much better. In short, if she is Ch'unhyang, Simch'ŏng, Changhwa and Hongryŏn (all female characters in old stories) in one, entirely welcome.

As for myself, I can be anything you might wish. I may be any age you want. I can change height by three feet reduce or gain about one *kwan* (3.75 kg) over night. I studied *One-thou-sand-character-primer* (a beginner's textbook of Chinese characters) at the age of three from my mother, and *Tong-mongsŏnsŭp* (a textbook more advanced than the former with moral and historical content) at the age of four from my father. I graduated from the Public School of Foreign Language in the capital at the age of twelve thereby adding a western flavor to my scholarship in traditional learning. Thus I became the mixing ball of oriental and western cultures and as a result can eat everything except the spawn of globefish.

I sent this advertisement out by as many routes as were accessible to me. Then, by the weekly, monthly, and yearly, three women applied. One of them Yŏngja was a woman who gave love. The next one Mija was a woman who took love. And the last, Sukja was one who couldn't decide where she belonged. This was the order in which the three women appeared to me. If they had come in a different order, that is, if the last one or the middle one had come first, or, if only the first one had come to me at the end, I am sure I would have hit it off with at least one of them. I will explain why.

At first, with the first woman, I wanted to give my love but she only knew to give love on her part and didn't know how to take it. So she went. After this, with the next woman, I felt like getting love instead of giving, but this one knew only to gobble up love and didn't know how to give. So with the third one, I used my head and alternated between giving and taking. She said I was restless, temperamental, and lacked manliness. She said I was just like herself and went away.

Hey, listen, look here, I called, and yet she went away.

(Rubs eyes)

What a disaster! Come back.

I became desperate. I was too desperate to think of who came first and who should have come last and what Yŏngja was like and what Mija lacked. It was all off the point with a man who couldn't even tell a pack of cigarettes from an ash tray. And by Jove it is tough to be sightless!

(A pause)
Kung-sang-kak-ch'i-u (five tones of music)
(A pause)
T'ae-Chŏng-T'ae-Se-Mun-Tan-Se (the first syllables of the names of the Yi dynasty kings, thus arranged for easy memorization by the school children)

With this sonorous voice, am I to starve and die like a piteous beggar? One day, however, I came across a man who was in the upper grade at my school. He was known to be well-read in genealogical rocords. So he said, don't you know that your tenth generation ancestor peddled stories? My ears stood up at this news and I cleaned up both my ears instantly to hear better.

(Sound of drum)
Never tell *Changhwa-Hongryŏn* in front of a stepmother.[2] If you must, turn Changhwa into Ch'unhyang and Hongryŏn into Simch'ŏng. If the stepmother's frown still remains, turn the stepmother into the tortoise of *Pyŏljubu-jŏn.*[3] If she still frowns, then I don't know. Never tell *Honggildong-jŏn*[4] in front of a dishonest government official and never tell the story of *Prince Sado*[5] in front of parents who have a crippled son. At a house where they have an ancestor with the zodiac of snake, do not tell *Yuch'ungyŏl-jŏn,*[6] but if you must, turn the snake into a dragon. *Ch'unhyang-jŏn*[7] and *Simch'ŏng-jŏn*[8] will do well enough under any circumstances. But the chance is your audience may think he can tell them better than you can. And that won't do because then the host and the guest will have changed places. O.K. I will keep at this in mind. And now I will be on my way, to success, and to fame!

(He strides forward briskly.)
Here comes a cripple, here comes a blind man. Make way, everyone, move over a little, you, too, mister. And now that I have found my rightful profession, I feel like having some real fun. I hear that my tenth generation grandpa was a mighty good dancer, too.

Hey nonny-no, hey hey

Look at that cripple dance
Tralalala Tralalala
(Performs a round of dance)
Hush, I see a nice plain broad face. Oh, I forgot I was blind.
What I meant was you all must be able to see my face clearly.
(Sound of drum)
When I was a maiden, I gave birth to eight babies, and after
I put up my hair (sign of womanhood) gave birth to five more
thus making the total thirteen. Other folks name their young-
sters Poksun, Pokhi, Oksun, Okja, and so on. But I named my
children in a way they would be easy to call, easy to remem-
ber, good to look at and nice to hear. I named them January,
February, March, April, May, June, July, August, September,
October, November and December. Nice and gay, aren't
they?
Why is one left?
The one that's left is Leap Month. But you don't know
where I gave my eldest daughter away.
I gave her to *Kwan.* [9]
You mean she became a government official?
I mean I gave her to the *Kisaeng-kwan* of the Tourist
Bureau. But you don't know where I gave away my second
daughter. I gave her away to *Pyŏk.*
Did you give her away to the Buddhist temple to do the
three-year *myŏn pyŏk* (wall-facing)?
Don't you know *Pyŏkje* (a place well-known for graveyard)
on the other side of Hongje-dong? I mean I sent her there as a
virgin. But you don't yet know where I gave my third daughter away. I gave her away as a girl of the year of *yang* [10] to
look toward the seas and the lands far away with her *ap'ro*
bra (one with fastening hook on the front side) waving on
her breast.
But now, let's see where my eldest daughter's husband is.
Aha, there he is, that one with the sky blue jumper on. Hey,
look here, son, why don't you greet your wife's mother?
(Gesturing with hand)

You don't know where my second daughter's husband is. Oh, there he is, my second daughter's husband. That one with the red shirt on. Look here, son, you don't have to blush because your wife's mother's having a little fun. But now, let's see where my youngest daughter's husband is. Oh, he is right here.

(He grabs a man who is sitting in the front row.)

Ay, ay, my son, you lost your teeth getting old.

My daughters and their husbands are all here, twenty six of them all together, and six times six is thirty six and six times three is eighteen. Wow, there are so many of you here and I am satisfied.

(He goes round making tapping sounds with his feet.)

I feel so good I don't feel like talking much. But I will sing. That tenth generation ancestor of mine, the one who lived in Suwŏn, he failed in the national examination for selecting government officials that was held in the capital. In addition, he spent the money his wife earned selling her warm lower section. Consequently he could not take the trip back home and in a fit of desperation decided to buy poison with the couple of pennies left and kill himself. He bought rat poison and walked back to his lodging with a horrible determination in his heart, tears in his eyes and sorrowful lamentations coming from his mouth:

One, I haven't learned one word or one number
Two, Tanch'ŏn is in Hamgyŏng province that's in the north
Three, two Marches make one leap March
Four, are the sycophants crazy or promiscuous?
Five, wife of five-*ch'on* (unit of classifying blood relations) uncle is called *Tangsukmo* (aunt)
Six, the road stretching inland is called *sinjangno* (meaning newly-made road)
Seven, the blue mountain of a seven precious stones is the land of Manchuria
Eight, the best mountain in eight provinces is Diamond

Mountain
Nine, the soup is boiling and the rice is simmering

Hey, Mister, we sit here because you said you would tell us stories and because you said you had a talent inherited from your ancestor; we don't want to hear any more of your number game.

Oh, that was so.

(A pause)

How far did I get?

I got as far as where my ancestor made up his mind to kill himself and with tears in his eyes lamented, right? Why cry, a grown man like him?

It's because there's so much harmful gas in the street these days. That's why there are tears in the eye. *A-i-go* (sound of keening, also an exclamation).

Look here, young man. I just said *a-i-go*, one time, and you sighed. Why was that?

It's because your story about your examination-taking ancestor wavers so much and is so poor and dull. How could I help sighing, then?

Don't talk like that because this grandpa of mine was a very special person. Years ago, during the time of Japanese Occupation, that is, this ancestor of mine was a great traveler. He went all over the country, even to the places in the north across the now demilitarized zone, Sŏngjin, Unggi, Ch'ŏngjin, Wŏnsan. He even went out on the sea. There was no place he wouldn't go. And all the time, he made it his occupation to whore and to chase the ghosts. So he knew how to use a few learned words. But he knew better how to use words of four letters. His cursing was the more picturesque because it was polished through years of chasing all sorts of street ghosts. He certainly knew how to use the most obscene language.

I grab and swish
The bamboo pipe with twelve joints
(Dance)

Hey, hey, what's that place called. It's called SSeoul. How come you talk obscenity all the time? ('SS' sound in Korean frequently associated with obscenities.) This won't do. So now I will cut short the story of my grandpa and come down to my father.

A proper man has to be gifted in body-speech-learning-judgment. That is, a man can become a village chief or a county chief if he has a good face and talks well. My father studied *Sijŏn, Sojŏn, Chuyŏk, Non-ŏ, Maengja, Yegi, Ch'un-ch'u, Taehak, Sohak* (Chinese classics), *Tongmongsŏnsŭp* and there fore could sing quite well. But he had one defect—he had moles on his face. For this reason he could not get a post in the government and spent his better days in the brothels. In his old age, he had no songs or books to sell any more except the *One-thousand-character-primer*. With this one book, he managed to make a living. He would compose invocations for the illiterate country people and in recompense receive a sack of rice or some such thing. This continued not a year or two but over ten years and more. It was a hard living all right. But as the old saying goes, there's a good time even for the grasshoppers. Because his life brightened up all of a sudden lately.

How?

It's like this. Of late, an amazing number of people are taking interest in *kisaeng* houses. My father teaches these lecherous men the rules about going to a *kisaeng* house. He is at his job 24 hours a day and earns money as fast as if he were printing it.

What, are there rules about going to a *kisaeng* house?

Ignorant fellow!.You must have come from another country. Get up at once and go to Ch'ŏnggyech'ŏn (name of a street that used to be a stream) and ask people where is the spot above which used to stand Supy'o Bridge. They will point to a hole in the middle of the street. Slip into it when nobody's looking and climb down. Look for Master Supy'o and bow low to him. He will be sure to ask, what did you think this place was? Then don't say you thought it was part of the sewage system running below Ch'ŏnggyech'ŏn or that it stank, or that it was noisy down there because of the vehicles running overhead. You shouldn't mention any of these things. You should just close your eyes profoundly and speak like this:

I have a request to make. If attendance to class is permitted, you will begin to take your course in the rules about the *ki-saeng* house. There will be three months of fast preliminary class and six months of regular standard class, nineteen months of studying altogether. After this period you will be told: "These are the Musts in going to such a place. Do not make light of them." You will, of course, have the sense to say: "I will not." Go now, quickly, too. And learn. Learn about Hwasaek, who has a pretty face, Wŏlhasŏn who has a good figure, Ponghaun who has talent in playing string instruments, Ch'uwŏl who has a good singing voice, Hongyŏn who fills a room with spring light, Kangsŏn who drops tears easily, Yŏmjusŏn who came from the monks quarters in Mt. Pong-rnae, Ŭmdŏk who is coquettish, Chajilye who is a *kisaeng* from Haengju and Waerang who has a good body and can sing old songs and is a good gogo dancer. They will be all there, standing in line in front of the hole in Ch'ŏnggyech'ŏn from which you are supposed to come up completely rotten after nineteen months.

What, are you laughing at me, rascal? It must be that you don't know anything about the faithful Ch'unhyang. Then listen to me:

(Sound of drum)

Now, isn't that just like her, my mad-woman of a wife! Strumming it off, like that, just when I was getting ready to begin, too! I hope she will be stuck with it to her dying days.

Just a minute. I think I will have a bowl of rice wine. Hey, you, bring it here.

(Sound of drum)

A glass of water came in, I grab the boy who brought it and:
Attention! At ease! Attention! At ease! Hey, cousin!

(Sound of drum)

What kind of answer is that? Don't tremble. Just answer. Loudly, cousin, loudly.

(Sound of drum)

I can't eat because there's no spoon. So I will push the bowl aside like this and begin the story of Ch'unhyang. But I hesitate because if I just tell the story as it is there may be someone among my audience who will say he can tell the story better. I will tell it in a language which only the singing and dancing groups such as the Group of the Begging Monks, the Group of Prostitutes, the Group of Key Makers, or the Palace Group, used between themselves, I mean the kind of language nobody else beside them can understand. So now, I will tell the story of Ch'unhyang in such a language. But where shall I begin?

The part in which Master Yi (hero of the story of Ch'unhyang) tops the national examination.

So I tread the soil of Namwŏn in an instant. Over Paksŏk Hill and beyond Japan I travelled and arrived at the house of Ch'unhyang. When I got there, I heard somebody praying in the back of the house: I pray, I pray, please help Master Yi of Samch'ŏng-dong pass the examination and please help him get the post either of governor or envoy to Chŏlla Province. Let him become either one and let him come to Namwŏn today and save my daughter Ch'unhyang.

After praying this way, the woman slumped down on the ground and said:

Ch'unhyang, my baby, my wicked, wicked daughter. How good to you was he, your *yangban* (aristocrat) lover? What are you doing to your old mother? My daughter who is about to die at such a tender age! Why didn't you get born somewhere else, to a different parent? Why did you have to be born to me, a worthless piteous woman? Are you dying for my sin? I raised you as if you were a jade leaf on a golden bough though you had no father. But what good is it to you when you are dying a death like this! Change the water on the altar, Hyangdan (a servant girl), because today will be the last day I can pray for my daughter.

Aha, I had thought I had become king's envoy thanks to my ancestors. But now I know that it was not so. Now I see that half of the work was the kindness of Buddha and the other half was my mother-in-law's prayer. The king's envoy got together with Ch'unhyang's mother and Ch'unhyang caught up with them. The woman said:

Come in, come, come right in.

She grabbed the young man by the hand with a face that showed how glad she was to see him back. And let's listen to what he said:

Trust me.

(Sound of drum)

What?

Trust me.

Tralalalalalala and trust me.

Tralalalalalala and join me.

Hey, what's this? You were going to tell us the story of Ch'unhyang not sing a stupid song, a western song at that! Is it because you are teaching the course on *kisaeng* houses that you sing western songs? Do you teach only western songs? I teach our songs also.

(Sound of drum)

Nebille Tungnyŏn, Maeksaek Sodaem, Ssanggame Sŏndung, Little daughter Big daughter, *T'ansil T'uksil*, all of you, look at me with round eyes the shape of the hole made with a stick and listen to me while I sing you the song of woman.

Listen, you girls, listen well,
While I tell you the duties of a woman.
When you are married to a man
Know that you are married to him by the will of heaven.
The happiness and hardship of a hundred years depend on this one man.
If you fail to win his love and lost it instead,

How are you going to sit alone in your cold empty room?
When your husband is dead,
You can at least hope to see him in dreams.
But if your husband leaves you,
He becomes your enemy for a hundred years.
He will give you the white of his eye when he sees you,
And he will slander you when he opens his mouth.
When the love is gone out of marriage,
Your husband becomes worse than a stranger.
Love once gone never returns,
Like the spilled water that never goes back into the bowl.
Daughter, daughter, baby daughter,
Be very very careful.
A husband is heaven and a wife is earth.
How can the earth stand eye to eye with heaven hundreds of
thousands miles above.
If he gets angry, you should smile,
And if he is worried, look apologetic.
Don't let him see things soiled,
And don't let him hear petty words.
Do not try to stop the will of heaven.
If a woman is strong and a man is weak,
It is going against the rules of nature;
You will lose your property
And meet a great misfortune.
It will be ruin for you and your house.
If a subject is loyal to the sovereign,
There's peace and prosperity in the country.
If a wife is wise and faithful,
There'll be wealth and happiness in the house.
Be good to him until he dies,
And be respectful to him even in old age.
Look ahead when you walk,
And think before you speak.
When you prepare food for the ancestral rites,
Take care not to let unclean things go near it.
Do not laugh in front of elders unless it's necessary.
Do not go out in the dark alone.
Do not clap your hands or laugh loudly at a gathering.

Do not take off your clothes in front of your husband.
If you can keep your body as whole as your parents gave it to you,
It will be the best sign of filial piety,
And high virtue in a woman.
Do not butt in when elders talk,
And do not lie down and take a nap.
Do not eat a snack every night,
And do not waste even the left-overs.
After your parents-in-law sit at table.

(Jumping onto the stage)

My third, fifth, seventh, and eighth ancestors must be wondering at me now. They must wonder why the descendant whom they raised as if he were a piece of jade is delivering the kind of speech a mother would tearfully deliver to a daughter who's getting married.

Am I then a pimp and not a teacher of the rules of a *kisaeng* house?

If I am left alone to fare as I will, I will be the disgrace of my ancestors and may take out the family tree to sell it for candy. And so, the ten generations of my ancestors gathered together on the day of ancestral rites and passed a proposal to punish me: they decided to cut off my uvula.

(Lights a match.)

Puff!

(Looks aside.)

Is he drunk?

When I lit another match, the old man who wanted to borrow a light was gone and a fishy smell was filling the air. I looked down at my palm and saw that it was covered with blood. Oh, my!

I walked and ran down the mountain slope but the tinkling sound followed me. Tinkle tinkle.

The sound was so clear and sonorous that I felt curious. I said to myself, it must be somebody's calf falling and turned back to look. I turned back again and again but as soon as I looked back the sound would go away to the far side of the field. But as soon as I turned my back to it, the sharp tinkling sound would hit my ear again. It seemed to be asking me questions such as these:

Tinkle. How is *O-li* (five li) different from a *Ori* (duck)?

For *O-li* (about 1.2 miles) goes to the market and the duck goes into the pot, I answered.

Tinkle. How is *komo* (aunt) different from *komu* (rubber)? I answered that *komo* is someone with the same last name and *komu* is something *komo* puts on her feet. (The reference is to rubber shoes worn by Korean ladies.)

Tinkle. How is a prayer different from a prayer?

A prayer takes you to heaven and a prayer to the *Samsindang* gets you a baby.[11] If a magpie crows you will have a guest and if a rooster crows the ghost will depart, I shouted these last words and as I did so it said it would go away and offered its hand for me to shake.

I looked at him hastily. Today is my *Chesa* (rite) day, so I am leaving with a full stomach. When you go back to your house, eat the rice with your spoon and heat the soup before you eat it. Did he leave any? Yes, for you to eat. So I said goodbye and walked on. But as I walked for some time, I heard footsteps right behind me.

(Makes sound of footsteps)

Who's this? I came back. Did you forget anything? I could not see my way ahead. Won't you walk with me some distance, just as far as Mu-ak Hill? Go ahead.

(Sound of drum. He writhes as if something is choking him.)

Oh, I am hurt. My throat! It's my uvula scoundrel.
Stop, give back my uvula. Give it back!

(He puts both hands on his throat and falls down to the ground. Sound of drum. He moves around the stage squeaking rat sounds. Then he adjusts the false teeth in his mouth and in a second recovers.)

Whew! I nearly became a ghost before I was dead, even. And just to sell a few pennies' worth of drug, too! Oh, my throat, kiak kiak.

Therefore those of you who can't see clearly, kiak, kiak, and who are no better than blind men, and those who get a heart-pounding like when watching a fire if somebody shouts, and those who stammer and those who get swollen uvulae at the slightest change of weather and cough when trying to speak, and those who have the stubborn idea that it is better to die rather than live a shameful life, none of you need try any more drugs either western or oriental any more. You don't need yoga or a shaman. Kiak, kiak. *(He takes a turn around the stage and produces from his pocket a small pill which is bigger than rat drug and smaller than the dumpling in red bean gruel.)* How can you claim that this will open the blind man Sim *pongsa*'s eyes or will give one a voice as if he swallowed an engine. You lie too much, despicable fellow, even if you are a drug-peddler. Some of you may say so. And so I won't claim that this will give sight to Sim *pongsa* or give you the voice of an engine. Then, what will this round little pill do for us, you may wonder.

It's neither eye, nor mouth but something that stands in the middle. It's the two holes of a nose. How can a nose see or speak? It cannot. It cannot see or speak, but it can tell one thing from another. Instead of a long explanation, I will put up a demonstration right here because, as the old saying goes, seeing once is better than hearing a hundred times. Even if some of you don't like what I am going to do, I beseech you to be patient with me because your having to be patient with me is inevitable in view of our destiny to meet each other here and now, etcetera.

(After mimicking a gesture of swallowing a pill, he moves into the spectators' seats.)

Aha, here's somebody who has just had a nice bowl of Chŏnju mixed rice. And here's one who ate a good dish of steamed fish-jaws of Masan. And this here gentleman, I am sure, ate the noodles of Ch'unch'ŏn and the gentleman next to him, wow, had it in fancy style. He had sliced raw sweet fish of Hwadong with sesame-leaf flavored with soy sauce. I bet the heart of that fish he ate kept on beating even after it was skinned. Now, do you all agree that I can smell rather well? Take this young lady here, for

instance. I know she had Myŏngdong cut noodles. And this uncle
here ate a bowl of Hamhŭng Body-building Soup at Wŏnnamdong, I am sure. And what's this! Here's a gentleman who had
sliced raw snake under the Big Bridge in Wŏnju! I think I will
stop the demonstration here. Anyhow, this is how good the drug
is. Just as you all saw right now, during my demonstration.
Didn't I tell the thing inside of you as if I had gone through it as
the thread goes through beads? Here's something else. One day,
after sharpening my nose with one of these pills, I chanced to
meet two people from my home town. One of them had come to
Seoul to visit the zoo and the other was working in Seoul as a taxi
driver at the airport.

How did I find out these things? You and I never met before.
Parathion. Parathion.

Do I stink?

Parathion. Parathion. I winked at him. He then believed me
and offered to buy me thick wine. At the tavern he told me the
story of the clerk in the Irrigation Cooperative who was haunted
at the grave of a virgin and died. As I listened I realized it was a
story about myself.

Come to think of it. I knew from the first you looked like him.
So, that's you, eh? But then, what happened? You can't have
opened the grave and come out alive. And then, if you are a
ghost, you can't look so complete and natural with everything in
its place. Your breath is regular and warm, and, that's right,
your pulse beat is strong.

It's like this. Making a living for myself and my widowed
mother, I lost whatever patch of land I borrowed from the
Irrigation Cooperative even though I clerked three years at the
Irrigation office. So I talked things over with my mother and
made a decision. I told my mother that I would pretend to be
dead at the grave of a virgin and told my mother to act her part.
I told her to spread the rumor of my death. I said it would be better than going to prison. I slipped out of the coffin before they
nailed it down and hid myself behind the folding screen for three
days. After that I came up to Seoul and became a drug-peddler,

becoming blind or dumb when necessary.

Heh, heh. *(He laughed.)*

Tinkle.

Oh, my nose! Let go of my nose! I said what I said just in order
to sell a few packs of drugs, but I never laid my eyes on you, sir.
Show me your birth certificate, sir. You and I have no reason to
meet, not even in the next world! Oh, my nose, let go of it, will
ya?

I smell something, I smell something. I smell thick rice water.
It must be the ghost of that virgin. They say you should chase the
thief but placate a ghost.

Dear lady who's picking the peas,

Are the ribbons at the end of your braid plain silk or patterned
silk?

What if it is silk!

I smell something again. What shameful deed did I commit in
my last life to have a ghost haunt my nose like this? Since things
took this turn, however, I will aside the four brothers and sisters
of ear-eye-mouth-nose but ask assistance of the four sisters and
brothers of my two hands and two feet. And with these I
descend. Those of you whose knees when you walk down the
steps make the sound of the wooden bell and hurt, duk, duk,
duk, and those of you whose elbows make the sound of doors
opening and shutting even when you bend them a little to drink a
cup of tea, squeak, squeak, to you I present this, the drug that
will cure you surely.

*(Mimics the gesture of swallowing a pill and also the gesture
of taking bodily exercise stretching arms and bending the body,
etc. After this he puts his palms together in the manner of a monk
and begins an incantation.)*

Omsalbamotjamojisadayasabaha

Omsalbamotjamojisadayasabaha

Omsalbamotjamojisadayasabahaburim

(Addressing his hands)

You're falling off, you're falling off, you're falling off, you're
falling off, you're falling off. . . .

(The hands separate.)
You're coming together, you're coming together, you're coming together, you're coming together. . . .
(The hands come together again.)
You're falling off, you're falling off, you're falling off. . . .
(The hands separate like before but one of them does not function properly.)
You're coming together, you're coming together, you're coming together. . . .
(The hands come together again.)
You're falling off, you're falling off, you're falling off. . . .
(The hans stay together. He seems dismayed at this unexpected happening. He scowls and groans as if he were sitting over the toilet pit.)
You're falling off, you're falling off, you're falling off, you're falling off. . . .
(The hands stay together to the end.)

CURTAIN

NOTES

1. Recently some merchants are rumored to have made a big sum of money selling red peppers as the price of red peppers went up suddenly.
2. Changhwa-Hongryŏn is an old story in which a good girl Hongryŏn is persecuted by her stepmother.
3. Another old folk tale about a clever rabbit who saves himself from the Dragon King of the ocean by using his wits. Tortoise acts as the Dragon King's emissary in the story.
4. A story of a just-minded young man Honggil-dong who rebels against the corrupt government officials.
5. Prince Sado is known to have been murdered by his father because of his mental frailty.
6. A war story of the Yi dynasty in which Yu Ch'ung-yŏl, a loyal subject, saves his king and the country from peril, but the writer's refer-

ence is to the folk belief that certain animals have totemic significance specific to certain families or clans.

7. A famous old love story. Ch'unhyang, the beautiful daughter of a former *kisaeng* marries a high government official after difficulty.

8. The story of Simch'ŏng, whose filial devotion to her blind widower father Sim *pongsa* (blind man) earns him new sight and herself the position of a queen.

9. *Kwan* has a double meaning of 'having a post in the government' and 'house.'

10. *Yang* has the double meaning of 'sheep' and 'the West.'

11. It is believed that if a childless woman prays at *Samsindang* (the shrine of the three founding gods of Korea), she will be given a child.

Getting Married

by Yi Kang-baek
translated by Sŏ Chi-mun

Characters

A man   *A woman*   *A servant*

Author's Note

   This play is written to be produced in a drawing-room or a small café theater. It is, so to speak, a chamber music play.
   There is no need to install a stage platform, neither is there much need for lighting and sound effects. What is absolutely necessary is the audience. The servant in the play should take the members of the audience as his masters. He should borrow from them such articles as a hat, a pair of shoes and a necktie. This is not simply to use them as stage properties. What is significant is that the articles are borrowed and then returned,

and the loan has a grave significance in the play.

The servant adorns the man with the borrowed articles. The man manages to look like a rich man with the help of the borrowed articles, though they don't exactly go together and some of them look preposterous.

The man is sitting leaning backward, and presently begins to read from a huge book which he is holding up, and which completely shields his face from view.

The servant stands beside the man in an upright, immobile posture. He is holding in his hand a pocket watch as big as a tray, which he sometimes actually uses as a tray. It is desirable that the servant, who frequently marks time scrupulously, look brusque and sturdy.

(The man reads.)

Once upon a time, which was a long time ago, there lived a swindler. He was young and handsome, but he was penniless. One day, he felt lonely and felt a longing to get married. Everyone is bound to feel lonely at one time in his youth. It is said that that's why everyone gets married. But the swindler had a great agony. His agony was this: what girl in this world would marry a penniless man like him? None. He thought there was none. This thought drove him to despair. He could not help sighing. That is not a pleasant feeling. Nor is it good for health—mentally or bodily. One must drive out such despair by deep breathing. The young swindler breathed deeply. And he got up resolutely.

Let us not sigh.
Let us not worry!
Leave all headaches to fate!
Let us enjoy this day
And never look back on the past.
Though all things may look sad,

They will turn to blessings for you.
All are as God disposes.
Let us follow God's will!

He roamed all day. And he borrowed a house with a garden,
splendid garments, and all the paraphernalia needed to make
him look like a rich man.

Blessed be the beauty of youth!
Blessed be the providence of God!

The young swindler's wish was fulfilled. He was able to borrow an imposing mansion with a garden, a hat and a necktie,
luxurious suits, and even this sturdy servant. But he had to
borrow them upon a condition. Each loan had a time limit. He
was to be master of this mansion for no more than forty-five
minutes, after which time he had to return it to its real owner.
The necktie he could wear for eighteen minutes, the hat for
nineteen minutes and fifty seconds, and so on. But the young
swindler was contented. And so, he looked up the women's
magazines and sent a telegram to a woman listed as looking for
a companion. The woman responded immediately. She said
she was willing to come to a rendezvous to see if they were
compatible as marriage companions. That was exactly what
he wanted. *(As if to himself)* Why isn't she here yet? *(Resumes
reading.)* The appointed time is already past. *(The servant,
his eyes upon the watch, holds up his hand with five fingers
spread.)* It was five minutes past the appointed time. He became anxious. He. tried to calm himself with reading. *(The
servant takes away the book without a word. It is a completely
mechanical movement, devoid of all feeling. All the servant's
gestures are mechanical throughout the play. When the man
makes as if to protest, the servant just brusquely thrusts before
him the pocket watch. Before the man has time to show that
he understands, the servant turns about and exits with the
confiscated article. A little later, the servant returns and takes*

up his immobile posture beside the man again.)
Look, have you got no mercy? *(The servant remains silent.)*
Oh, I forgot. You don't speak. Your master told me.
"I'll lend him to you. But don't ask any questions of him.
This servant never answers anything," your master said. I
almost forgot that. But I wonder what's the matter with the
girl? *(He takes a look at the servant's watch.)* It's already getting to be ten minutes past the appointed time. Oh, I can't
bear to have my precious life wasted like this. *(The man paces
among the audience with an agonized expression. He stops suddenly and accosts a woman in the audience, with a smile, as if
an idea had dawned upon him.)* Yeah! That may be it! Is it
true that women are like that? That they keep men waiting for
about five minutes so they may look prettier? But this is too
much. Could she be a real beauty? Could that be why she
keeps me waiting twice as much as women usually do? Well,
it'd be worth the waiting if the woman's as pretty as you. If she
were, I could wait not only ten minutes but even twenty
minutes. *(The man comes back to his chair and sits down. He
fretfully smoothes his clothes and repeatedly takes off and puts
on his hat. He finally takes off his hat, puts it down on the
table and springs up. He steals a look at the servant's watch.
He swallows. Then he walks up to a man in the audience.)* I
can't stand this. Would you lend me a cigarette? I'm not asking for a donation. I'm simply asking for a loan. Oh, thank
you. Eh, this is Milky Way. *(To another man in the audience)*
Have you got a Blue Celadon? Well, let me borrow one. *(The
man takes out from his pocket a flat, empty cigarette packet
and fills it with cigarettes borrowed from the men in the audience.)*
Do any of you have Fountain? Fountain? I heard it's a new
brand and has a fresh taste. Well, *Hansando* isn't bad either.
And let me borrow a Pagoda, too, if any of you happen to have
one. Well, I'm not exactly a cigarette collector. It's just to lull
my impatience. *(He lights up a cigarette.)*
Take a look at this lighter. It's most expensive. It's un-

necessarily made of gold and has pearls stuck in it.

(To the servant) Hey, how long is this supposed to be mine? *(The servant sticks out one right finger and four left fingers.)* I see. Now that about ten minutes have passed, I have about four more minutes to own this. But it's still completely mine. My lighter. One that's made of gold, with pearls stuck in it. It must be certain that I'm rich. This luxurious possession proves it. Be that as it may, thank you all for the cigarettes. We must all help one another, right? In that sense, could I borrow just one more? *(A knocking sound is heard.)* Did you hear that? *(The servant remains speechless.)*

Hey, isn't someone knocking? *(The servant doesn't even give him a glance.)* Hurry and open the gate. *(The servant is silent.)*

Well, there's no help. I'll have to go and open the gate myself. *(The man opens the gate. A woman enters.)*

The servant is over there. I'm the master. *(The woman runs over to the servant and makes a greeting.)*

The master is over here. Over here. *(The woman, embarrassed, runs back to the man. The man gazes at the woman as if she had been a fine art piece and walks round her two or three times.)*

I knew it.

The woman: You knew. . . what?

The man: Yes. I knew. That you are beautiful. There are ways of knowing. The longer the woman keeps you waiting, the more beautiful she is. Yes! Time is an accurate gauge in that respect. Of course, it's a useless gauge if the result is bad. Do you mind if I smoke? *(The man sticks a cigarette in his mouth and takes out the lighter. He feels like showing off. He throws up the lighter in the air and catches it two or three times.)*

You see this lighter? It's most expensive. And it has genuine pearl decoration. *(The servant catches the lighter thrown up in the air.)*

Give it back! *(The servant points at his watch.)*

Already? The four minutes are already up? Time does fly.
(To the woman) Where did you put it?
The woman: Where did I put what?
The man: My lighter.
The woman: Your lighter?
The man: Er. . . . No. I mean your wings.
The woman: Wings!?
The man: Yes, your wings. Of course you left them at home.
   I hear that modern angels are so modest they tend to leave
   their wings at home. I suppose you are the same. *(Before the
   woman has time to say anything)* What I mean is, you are
   an angel even though you have no wings. Furthermore, in
   point of the right of possession, you are my angel. To
   repeat, you are mine. That's my point.
The woman: You have already reached that conclusion?
The man: (Decisively) Yes. As you have just heard.
The woman: It's too early to decide.
The man: Why? You don't like my conclusion?
The woman: It isn't that, but. . . we haven't even introduced
   ourselves. How do you do?
The man: How wonderfully do you do?
The woman: My name is. . . .
The man: Oh, let us put off introductions for the moment.
   These days human relationships begin with the conclusion
   and end with the introduction. That is the new custom.
The woman: Has such a custom come into being?
The man: Yes. That's the strategy a poor man uses when he
   meets a woman he falls in love with at first sight. If he
   introduces himself first, the woman's bound to be disappointed. Then, how could there be a relationship? The
   woman'd simply walk away. I would like to avoid such a
   misfortune. I would like our relationship to be enriched
   first, and then we can introduce ourselves. Wouldn't you
   like that, too?
The woman: (As if hypnotized) Yes, I'd like that, too.
   (The man and the woman sit down. The man proposes

immediately.)

The man: Will you marry me?

The woman: Marry. . . you?

The man: Yes! Marry me!

The woman: But we've only just met.

The man: If you want to talk about time, I, too, have something to say about that. Do you know how much of my time you've wasted? Of course you couldn't know. Ask the ladies and gentlemen here. You've wasted one third of the golden hours of my life!

 (The servant suddenly swoops down on the man and pulls off the man's shoes. The woman is aghast. The man tries to stave off the servant, but the servant points to his watch. The servant takes away the shoes.)

The man: Please forgive my servant's rudeness.

The woman: What's the matter?

The man: My shoes have left my feet. It's because time has passed.

The woman: I don't understand.

The man: Of course you don't. How could you understand that such is life?

The woman: What do you mean, such is life?

The man: Oh, well, don't try to understand.

 Women fall in love with men because they don't know that such is life, and men fall in love with women because they know it.

The woman: (Feeling dizzy) I'm getting confused. . . .

The man: That's right. Please do get confused.

The woman: May I have a glass of water?

The man: Of course. *(To the servant)* Hey, bring a glass of water. *(The servant stands immobile.)* Well, lend me a glass of water, then. *(The servant brings a glass of water.)* I see. I am to borrow even a glass of water. *(To the woman)* Here, drink this.

The woman: Thank you.

The man: You're welcome. I've borrowed it myself. *(The*

woman drinks the water.) Does that help?

The woman: Not much. I'm still confused.

The man: (Smiling) You'll get used to it.

The woman: To tell you frankly, I never even dreamed you could be so rich. I followed the directions on your telegram, and arrived at this magnificent house. I hesitated a long time before the gate.

The man: You should have had no fears.

The woman: It wasn't because of fears, but because of joy that I hesitated.

The man: (Smiling) Oh, you were ecstatic?

The woman: Yes. When your telegram came, my mother told me, "Go. Go, and if it's a poor man, make haste and come back, but if it's a rich man, be sure to grab him."

The man: What did you say to that?

The woman: I said, "I will, mother," holding up my right hand.

The man: You held up your right hand? An oath?

The woman: Yes.

The man: Is there any water left in the glass?

The woman: No. I drank it all.

The man: I wish you'd left some for me.

> *(The servant swoops down on the man and unties his necktie. The man struggles to stave him off, but the servant is too strong for him. The servant exits with the tie. The woman is aghast at the struggle.)*

The woman: What's the matter?

The man: (Gasps for breath but is smiling.) This time, the necktie has left my neck.

The woman: (Uncomprehending) What?

The man: There's no reason for surprise. It's just that time is up. But take heart in the thought that it's the necktie that has left my neck, and not vice versa. *(To divert the attention of the woman who is gazing at him embarrassedly)* Be that as it may, your mother sounds very interesting. I've gotten to be very interested in your mother. I'd like to hear more about her. What is she like? Is she generous? Why do you keep looking at me like that?

The woman: Your necktie. . . .

The man: I'm not interested in that.

The woman: Why was it taken away from you? *(Eyeing the servant who has returned and has taken up his immobile posture again)* And so brutally?

The man: That's it. Brutally. I'm not interested in servants who treats their masters brutally. I'm more interested in your mother's character. Whether she's generous or. . . .

The woman: But I'm concerned about the. . . .

The man: I know. The tie. Well, it won't be hard to get it back. *(To the servant, loudly)* Hey, bring it back! *(The servant does not answer. The man walks to him on tiptoe and whispers in his ear.)* Hey, let me borrow it for five more minutes! *(The servant does not answer.)* Please, just five more minutes! I beg of you! *(The servant remains unresponsive.)* All right. All right.

The woman: What does he say?

The man: Well, that I should manage without his help. *(The man walks among the audience and sits down in front of a man wearing a necktie.)* Well, of course he didn't say that. The cold-blooded servant doesn't have enough humanity even to say that. But why should I be let down by that? He's only a servant, after all. My pride is hurt, but as you must know that already, there's no need to repeat it. Well, let me tell you something. That's a real chic necktie you're wearing. Elegant color, refined pattern. Would you, by any chance, let me borrow it for five minutes? Just five minutes, no more. Would you? *(Borrows it from the man and puts it on.)* Thank you. I'll take good care of it while I borrow it. I'll keep in mind this is yours, not mine. Of course, it may be that you have borrowed it from someone else yourself. Anyway I'll use it carefully and return it to you. Well, you mark the time and let me excuse myself. *(The man returns to the woman hurriedly.)* Now, what do you think?

The woman: I think you look well.

The man: (Smiling) You're joking.

The woman: No, I mean it.

The man: (Turning to the man in the audience who lent him the tie) I render this glory unto you. *(Turning to the woman)* Well, let's get back to our original subject.

The woman: Where were we?

The man: Your mother. That's as far as we have gotten.

The woman: (With a small sigh) Well then, it'll be a long time before we get to me.

The man: That's right. I'd like to hear about you first, but that'd be disrupting the order. First the mother, and then the daughter. Isn't that the order? Well, let's proceed. I ask this out of a sense of obligation. What is your mother's character? Is she fierce, or is she gentle?

The woman: It's hard to say.

The man: Come on. Let's get it over with.

The woman: She's both gentle and fierce. *(The man puts a hand on his forehead.)* What's wrong?

The man: Nothing. I feel blocked. It seems so difficult. I know that winning you can't be very easy. I heard that even those who fall in love at first sight have to overcome many trials before they can get married. We are only at the threshold of our acquaintance. And we're still on your mother.

The woman: You mustn't be discouraged.

The man: I'll try.

The woman: You'd be surprised to hear this.

The man: Please go ahead.

The woman: I was born into this world.

The man: I'm surprised. So suddenly!

The woman: Yes. It's always so suddenly that one gets born. It was so suddenly that I don't know how I felt when I was born. Anyway, I was born, like that. And, do you know what my nickname used to be? It was, "wen."

The man: "Wen"?

The woman: Yes. Wen. You know, the unnecessary protuber-
ance. My father gave my mother love, and a wen. So,
that's what I was, a wen. There's something in that word
that creates a longing. A wen. When the wen was born, my
father fled. That is to say, he took to his heels. Later on,
my mother found out that he was a swindler and the great
fortune that he showed her was a temporary loan.

The man: A wen, a wen, a wen!

The woman: Yes. But I harbor no resentment againt my
father. There's something about him that creates a longing
in me, like in the nickname "wen." I wonder if that isn't
what he was born, himself. What do you think?

The man: A wen, a wen, a wen!

The woman: Yes, a wen! It may be unfair to my mother, but I·
like the fact that I'm a wen. It makes me feel. . . free. My
mother gets angry when I talk like this. That's only
natural. She's had so many hardships to bring up a wen all
by herself. Shall I talk about something else?

The man: No, please tell me more about it.

The woman: So, my mother is fiercely determined. She'll
never give me away to a swindler. I understand how she
feels.

The man: I can understand, too.

The woman: Thank you.

The man: You're very welcome.

The woman: Well, it's the first time I ever talked like this with
anyone. I haven't told anyone that I'm a wen. I had the
fact buried deep in my heart. You must have seemed ex-
traordinary kind.

The man: "Wen"?

The woman: Yes?

The man: Nothing. I. . . didn't mean anything.

The woman: Didn't the tone of your voice mean anything,
either?

The man: No, it didn't. (*The man stands up, unties his tie and
goes to the man in the audience he borrowed it from. His*

eyes are wet as he hands the tie back to the owner.) Here,
I return it to you as I said I would. I kept my promise to the
minute. But I wonder why I'm sad, all of a sudden? *(Paces
among the audience and talks to himself.)* Wen, wen, wen,
I love you. Wen, wen, wen, I love you.

The woman: What are you doing over there?

The man: (Still talking to himself) Wen, I love you.

The woman: (Walking up to the man) What are you doing?

The man: Wen, I'm thinking about what my property would
amount to.

The woman: Do you have to think about money at a time like
this?

The man: That is the stingy habit of a rich man. But, I've decided that I'm not going to think about my property since
it's so huge. How does that sound?

*(The woman leans her head on the man's shoulder. A
minute's pause. The servant walks up to the man threat-
eningly. The man is frightened. He does not want the
woman to see him thus.)*

The man: Close your eyes.

The woman: They're already closed.

The man: I'm happy.

The woman: So am I.

*(The servant lays his hands on the man. He fishes in the
man's pocket and goes out with all his possessions.)*

The man: This time, many trivial trinkets are leaving me. But
I grow happier. *(The woman, her eyes still closed, just
keeps smiling.)*

The man: Yes, dear wen. Many things, innumerably many
things have left me. That's not surprising. It's only that
time has passed. Some trees never say a word after returning thousands and thousands of leaves. Wen, I once had a
pet kitten. The kitten grew old, and when the time was up,
it returned its life without a complaint. Wen, I think I
have discovered a truth. Yes, wen, I know why leaves all
fall in the autumn. Now I have something to be proud of.

That is that I have learned that truth. I suppose that's the
only thing I can be proud of.

The woman: You're too modest.

The man: Not at all. Wen, do you have anything to be proud
of?

The woman: Yes, of course. Do you want to take a look?

The man: Yes, please let me take a look.

> *(The man and the woman return to the table. The
> woman opens her purse lying on the table and takes out
> three large photographs of women's faces. The servant
> takes a look at his watch and takes away the man's hat
> that has been lying on the table.)*

The man: This time, my hat has left the table. Isn't it fortunate? The hat is small, and the table is big. Think what
a loss it would have been if the table had left the hat.

The woman: Take a look at these.

The man: What are they?

The woman: They're photographs of me, my mother, and my
grandmother. They prove that the women in my family
are all beautiful. *(The man spreads the photos on the table
and gazes at them. The servant turns and shoots a glance at
the photos.)*

The man: (*Pushing the servant away*) How dare you? (*To the
woman*) You are the most beautiful of the three.

The woman: That's because I'm the youngest.

> *(The man lifts up the woman's photograph, holds it up
> beside the woman's face, and takes a long look.)*

The man: So, this is you at this moment?

The woman: Yes.

The man: May I ask how old you are?

The woman: Twenty-two.

The man: Twenty-two. That's the most beautiful time of life.
*(The man takes up this time the woman's mother's photo-
graph and holds it up beside the woman's face.)* A little
time has passed. What will become of you, then?

The woman: I will become a little old.

The man: Then, this will be your face. How old are you?

The woman: (A little huskily) Forty-five.

The man: Forty-five. You're at middle age. *(The man holds up the woman's grandmother's photo beside the woman's.)* More time has passed. This is your face, now. How old are you?

The woman: (Huskily) I'm over seventy.

The man: Over seventy? That's old. *(The man puts down the photographs on the table.)* That was an interesting game, wasn't it?

The woman: Yes, it was.

The man: As you may have guessed, the funny part was the passing of time.

The woman: (Pointing at the photos) But, don't you think they're pretty? The test of a beauty is whether she is beautiful even when old.

The man: That's true. Well said. The real fun lies in transcending time. Time! Let it pass. What do we care? We have our fun. Wen, you are beautiful, and you know what real fun is. Wen, I am completely ravished. Ah! I'm hardly myself now.

The woman: It's the same with me.

The man: I'm in ecstasy!

The woman: So am I!

The man: That's it! Life can be this ecstatic, depending on what attitude we take. But, wen, if, at this moment *(Pointing to the servant marking time on the watch)* this stout servant takes off my clothes. . . .

The woman: Why would he take off your clothes?

The man: If. . . I mean if?

The woman: But he shouldn't take off your clothes.

The man: Still, if he takes off my clothes, what will you do? Will you break off this fun, this ecstasy?

The woman: (Confused) Well. . . .

The man: Is it true that what is true is eternal?

The woman: Well. . . .

The man: Well then, let's put it to the test. (*The man's jacket is already being stripped by the servant. The woman, confused, keeps saying "well. . . ." The servant goes out with the jacket.*) Isn't it lucky? I still have my pants on.

The woman: Your pants. . . .

The man: Yes. Although I'm barefooted and jacketless, I'm not ashamed to say I love you. Let me propose to you formally. Will you marry me?

The woman: Why do you keep such a rude servant? Why don't you fire him at once?

The man: The servant has done nothing wrong.

The woman: He keeps stripping you because you keep him.

The man: He isn't stripping me. It's only that I'm returning those things.

The woman: You're too gentle.

The man: Well, I don't know if I'm gentle or not, but I do think my conduct is praiseworthy. My love for you hasn't diminished one bit even though I'm returning all these things one by one. On the contrary, my love is growing. My angel! No, my wen! My love had been dispersed among trinkets like shoes and necktie and hat and clothes. But now, my love flows to you, and only you! Will you accept my proposal?

(*The servant returns and plants himself before the man and the woman.*)

The woman: My God, he's here again!

The man: Don't bother. I'm not going to interfere with his carrying out his duty.

The woman: His duty? What's his duty?

The man: To take back the things I borrowed from his master. (*The servant hands the man an envelope. The man takes out a note from the envelope, reads it, and silently hands it over to the woman.*)

The woman: "Get out!" What does that mean?

The man: Well, it's a notice from the owner. He demands that I leave this house because the time's up.

The woman: Then, wasn't this house yours?

The man: I have nothing in the world that's mine. *(The woman staggers from shock.)* All these I had on loan. The full moon over there, the silver clouds, this friendly breeze, and maybe even myself and you. All I had temporarily, on loan.

The woman: Temporarily, on loan?

The man: Yes. Just so. *(The servant brings one enormous shoe, squats down, and puts it on his foot. He looks as if he is making ready to kick the man out with that foot.)* Marry me! I'll only love you while I have you on loan.

The woman: Oh, god! What can I do? *(The servant has finished tying the shoestrings.)* What about my oath? How can I take back my oath? The oath I swore to my mother, holding up my right hand?

The man: The oath! Well. . . . *(Gathers up the pictures on the table and hands them to the woman.)* Let's show these to your mother. When time passes, what remains to the man is love, and what remains to the woman, but three pictures? The pictures, of a young woman, of a middle-aged woman, and of an old woman. Your mother would understand.

The woman: No, she wouldn't understand. Not my mother. (She opens her purse and puts the pictures in it sadly and despairingly.) Thank you for an enjoyable day. It *was* an enjoyable day. It was the first time I. . . . Well, good bye. *(The woman walks up to the gate.)*

The man: Just one moment, wen! (The woman halts, but her face is averted.) You're leaving me? *(The woman does not respond.)* Give me one more minute.

The woman: *(Without resentment)* You are a swindler.

The man: Yes, I'm a swindler. I borrowed from the world some things. And I had to return them one by one when the time was up. Now, I'm stripped and revealed for what I am. But, wen, ask these people here. Ask if anyone has anything he can really call his. There's no one who truly owns anything. No one! Everyone has just borrowed things temporarily. One's eyes, nose, mouth, everything, they're all borrowed possession. *(Grabs a member of the audience at random and pointing to a thing he has.)* It that yours? What's the appointed time for this? Well, you take good care of it and return it good when the time's up. You see, my dear wen?

(The woman, her face still averted, walks out the gate. The servant slowly approaches, dragging his heavy foot. The man retreats with backward steps. The man pleads, like one on his last breath.)

Wen, I have nothing. All my things were borrowed possessions. But how about you, wen? What do you have? What have you got that's really yours?

(To the man in the audience who had lent him the necktie) Listen to me. You'll understand. When I borrowed your necktie, how did I handle it? Did I handle it roughly? Did I ruin it? No, I did not. I cherished it and then returned it to you. Wen, did you hear me? Here's my witness. I swear before this witness that I'll cherish you and love you for as long as I borrow you in this life and then, when the time's up, respectfully return you. Wen, you're my precious wen in this life. Wen, wen, wen! Can't you hear me?

(The man is kicked by the servant. The woman can't stand it any more and runs back to him, helps him to his feet and hugs him.)

The woman: Stop!

The man: Do you love me, now?

The woman: Yes! Who else would I love?

The man: Let's hurry and get married. Before I get kicked again!

The woman: Yes, let's. I heard that in this way my mother married a swindler, too.

The man: Come on, let's hurry!

The woman: Yes, let's hurry.   **CURTAIN**

*Author's note: The verses quoted are from *The Arabian Nights' Entertainment*.

Wha... i, Whai, a Long Long Time Ago

by Ch'oe In-hun
translated by Cho O-gon

Characters

Wife
Husband
Neighbor Woman, the mother of Kaettong
Old woman
Villager I and II
Policeman I, II, and III

Author's Note

1. This play is based on a legend from North P'yŏngan Province.
2. In the original legend, however, the story ends at the point when the baby is pressed to death under the grain sacks.
3. The symbolic structure of this legend is not only similiar to

that of the life of Jesus—the arrival of the absolute man, his short life in this world, the religious martyrdom, and his ascension to heaven—but also it resembles the origin of Passover in the Old Testament.

4. This play should be read as a common human tragedy without religious biases.
5. In the production, the dialogue and stage movements must be slow in order to create an atmosphere of uncertainty and hesitation, for this type of tragedy cannot be interpreted in a rational way.
6. This play should manifest the dark side of man who is neither capable of correcting nor distinguishing his own fate.
7. The characters in the play should appear as though they are puppets, manipulated by the lighting and music, and, in particular, by the director.
8. At the end of play, all the characters on stage should dance as though they are in a state of ecstasy without regard to the circumstances or the events in the play.

ACT I

A grass hut. Snowing. Early evening. The Wife is sewing under the dim light of an oil lamp. She is pregnant. She looks about fifteen years old. She might be even slightly younger than fifteen. Once in a while, she picks up her needlework and holds it as though measuring it with her eyes.

There is almost no household furniture. The Wife sits on the floor of the room. There is an oil lamp and fire pot. That is all.

Occasionally, the Wife picks up her needlework. Then she gazes at something with vacant eyes. Now she looks down at her abdomen.

She caresses her abdomen gently.

The sound of someone approaching is heard.

She listens carefully.

The sound of the wind.
She resumes her needlework.
She raises the wick in the oil lamp with her needle.
The sound of an owl hooting.
She listens carefully.
She examines the stew kettle in the fire pot.
She gathers the embers up and arranges with the fire tongs.
She resumes her needlework.
The sound of someone approaching.
She listens carefully.
The sound of the wind.
She listens carefully.
The sound of the wind.
She stands up and walks out of the room onto the wooden floor porch. Then she walks down to the yard.
She walks toward an imaginary gate. Then she looks into the distance in the darkness.
The snow falls on her head.
The sound of the wind.
The sound of an owl hooting.
(A pause)
She begins to walk slowly back to the room.
As she hears the sound of someone approaching, she turns around.
(A pause)
She returns to the room.
She raises the wick in the oil lamp.
She picks up her needlework.
Occasionally, she stops her needlework.
She caresses her abdomen.
She smiles.
The sound of the wind.
The sound of an owl hooting.
She raises her head and listens carefully.
The sound of someone approaching.
She stands up.

The Husband walks into the yard. He carries two grain sacks, one on top of the other, on the A-frame on his back. He takes the A-frame off his back and lets it stand near the edge of the wooden floor porch.

The Wife helps him. She brushes the snow off his shoulders. He shakes his shoes.

She brushes the snow off his trousers.

Their movements are slow as though their entire concentration is centered on these activities to the exclusion of all else. Each line of the dialogue is delivered slower than in usual conversation. The Husband has a severe stutter and speaks extremely slowly.

Conversation between the Wife and the Husband appears to stagnate. But the couple are accustomed to this slow situation. There are usually long and frequent pauses. It appears that a great deal of strength is needed to communicate with each other even for matters of no importance.

Wife: I suppose the road was slick.

Husband: A li. . . li. . . little.

Wife: (*Touching the grain sacks*) Everything went well, did it?

Husband: I plea. . . plea. . . pleaded the case. . . (*He unloads the grain sacks from the A-frame and puts them on the wooden floor porch.*)

Wife: (*Touching the grain sacks*) Millet and soybeans. . . .

Husband: Ye. . . Ye. . . Yea. . . .

Wife: Come in quickly. You must be very hungry. You haven't had anything to eat since you had that morsel for breakfast this morning. (*She carries a sack into the room.*)

Husband: Le. . . le. . . leave them alone. (*She continues to carry it. Roughly.*) I said le. . . le. . . le. . . leave them alone. I told you that you shouldn't ca. . . ca. . . ca. . . carry anything heavy. (*He takes the grain sack away from his wife.*) That, that is enough.

(*They look at each other.*)

Wife: Yōbo. * Sit down here and warm yourself. (*She pushes the fire pot to the place on the floor nearest the fireplace [the seat of honor]. She tends the stew kettle on the fire pot.*)

Husband: That's all. . . all. . . all. . . all right.

Wife: (*Setting the tables*) Sit down here.

Husband: Ju. . . just a minute. Sit down he. . . he. . . he. . . here.

Wife: Yōbo. I am in the room all the time.

Husband: (*Disurbed*) I said si. . . si. . . si. . . sit down here. (*The Wife gives in and sits down on the floor nearest the fireplace. She sets the table.*)

Wife: You must be hungry. (*The Husband opens one of the grain sacks and dips a bowlful of millet.*) *Yōbo!* (*He ties up the neck of the sack.*) What are you doing? (*He stands up with the bowl of millet. As she stands up.*) With that. . .!

Husband: Sit down qu. . . qu. . . quietly. I will cook a bowl of mi. . . mi. . . millet for you. You have a. . . a. . . almost given birth to a baby without having a single bowl of rice.

Wife: Are you crazy? How can we eat the seed millet? We need it for planting.

Husband: That is a. . . a. . . all right. Any way, we can pay it back in the f. . . fall. What difference does it make? We have a chance to eat a bo. . . bowl of cooked millet. I will cook it for you quickly.

Wife: Aigo. * *Yōbo,* give it back to me.

Husband: I told you there is no p. . . p. . . problem.

Wife: But it isn't right. Give it back to me. How can I possibly eat seed millets as if I'm going to give birth to a prime minister?

Husband: Ha! Le. . . le. . . leave me alone!

Wife: No. (*While she struggles to take the millet bowl away from her husband, she spills it on the floor.*) *Aigo.* What

---

* Yōbo: dear or my dear.
* *Aigo:* Good heavens.

shall I do? Aigo. *(She crouches and picks up the grains one by one.)* Aigo. You must be hungry. *(Pointing to the fire pot)* Yŏbo, the stew is burning. *(She gathers the ashes on the burning charcoal.)* Please, eat it quickly. *(The Husband turns around and picks up the millet from the floor. She now puts the gathered millet in the sack. Then she pushes her husband towards the floor nearest the fireplace and makes him sit down.)* Well.

Husband: *(He sits at one end of the small low table and signals his wife to sit down at the other end of it.)* The her. . . her. . . herb porridge. . . This is only mo. . . mo. . . mountain herb porridge. . . Yŏbo.

Wife: No. No. *(She sits down in front of the grain sacks in order to prevent his approaching them. The Husband begins to eat the herb porridge at last. Now the couple eat together. As she caresses one of the grain sacks.)* Now everything is all right.

Husband: *(Silence)*

Wife: Yŏbo, you must be worrying about something.

Husband: . . . . No. . . nothing. No. . . No. . . .

Wife: Nothing? There must be something. Do you have anything to worry about?

Husband: I said nothing.

Wife: Oh, my. . . I am frustrated.

Husband: . . . .

Wife: . . .

Husband: . . .W. . .w. . . well. A thi. . .thi. . . thief came down to the other vi. . .vi. . .village from the mountains.

Wife: A thief. . . did you say a thief?

Husband: He set f. . f. . . fire to the government building and s. . . s. . . stole grain from the warehouse.

Wife: Aigumŏni.*

Husband: There was a pu . . . public notice which said that we ought to report the appearance of any stranger in the

* Aigumŏni: a synonym for aigo.

village to the government . . . including every single strange shadow of a man . . . since we don't know when thieves will appear.

Wife: This happens every year. . . . It is nothing new.

Husband: By . . . by the way, I saw the head of a captured thief. It was hung high in front of the government building.

Wife: (As she clicks her tongue) Whether one starves to death . . . or is killed, . . . what difference does it make?

Husband: He harmed the government only to survive.

Wife: That is right.

Husband: Do you . . . do . . . do you know?

Wife: How . . . am I . . . supposed to . . . know . . . what?

Husband: What a strange thing to happen on this earth? Do you remember the . . . the . . . the sa . . . sa . . . salt peddler who brought a scabby infected do . . . do . . . donkey here?

Wife: . . . Yes.

Husband: The . . . the . . . the . . . sa . . . sa . . . sa . . . sa . . . sa . . . sa . . . sa . . . salt peddler.

Wife: Is this about him?

Husband: Tha . . . tha . . . tha . . . that is right.

Wife: Really?. . . That. . . consumptive who coughed a lot?

Husband: Re . . . re . . . re . . . really. That is strange.

Wife: Oh, . . . good heavens . . . . He sat on the edge of the wooden floor porch. . . while coughing and coughing.

Husband: Well, tha . . . that is right.

Wife: He . . . set fire . . . to the government building, did he?

(The sound of someone approaching. Silence. The sound of snow falling from a tree branch.)

Husband: (Quietly) No. . .no. . . nothing. It is no. . . no. . . nothing, isn't it?

(The Wife listens carefully directing her ears in the direction from which the strange sound has occurred. She goes towards the door and looks out at something in the dark. She holds on to her husband.)

Wife: I. . . don't. . . thank. . . there is anything.

Husband: Ūng.

Wife: (As she removes the ashes from the charcoal in the fire pot) What can they possibly steal from us. . . We don't have anything. *(Suddenly she turns around and looks at the grain sacks. She stops talking.)*

Husband: (Quickly. Towards the outside. Loudly) That. . . tha. . . that. . . is right! O. . . o. . . o. . . of course, the noble thi. . . thi. . . thi. . . thi. . . thi. . . thieves g. . . g. . . g. . . g. . . g. . . go only to the places that deserve their visits. That. . . tha. . . that is right. Right!

Wife: You have said well. You are right. . . . There is no source of worry in our house. We have nothing to worry about. That is good.

(A pause. The snow continues to fall. The couple sit down stiffly. Finally they relax. The howling sound of a wolf. The couple direct their ears in the direction from which the howling sound of the wolf is heard.)

Wife: This . . . this must be the last snow of the year. I think . . . .

Husband: Since we have had plenty of s. . . s. . . snow thi. . . this winter, I hope we will have a g. . . g. . . good ha. . . harvest in the fall.

Wife: For mercy's sake, I hope so.

Husband: But there will be an e. . . e. . . extra mo. . . mouth. So. . . .

Wife: I don't think the baby will eat too much for the first couple of years . . . I don't think so.

Husband: It is said that during a famine year adults may starve to death while children die by bursting their stomachs with overeating. Haven't you heard this?

Wife: This must happen when they drink too much water. . . . Well, . . . That must take place only in a fortunate village. *(She caresses her abdomen.)* If the baby were born in this . . . starving world,. . . it would have to struggle for survival . . . . What a pity.

Husband: Our way of li . . . living has not been di . . . different from that. When did we live better than that? We have always been grubbing ea . . . ea . . . ea . . . earth worms. Everything is pre . . . predetermined by the heavenly deity.

Wife: Yōbo, I wish I could stay as I am now . . . . That would be nice.

Husband: . . .

Wife: Without giving birth to the baby. . . .

Husband: . . .

Wife: Then the baby . . . wouldn't have to . . . suffer in this world, . . . not yourself . . . . You have even tried to cook seed millet for me,. . . . since I am pregnant. . . . When can I live in such luxury, . . . if I am not pregnant?

Husband: Have you ever hea . . . hea . . . heard of a co . . . co. . . co. . . conceived baby staying in the mother's womb forever?

Wife: Well. No . . . . That is true. But . . . .

Husband: The . . . the . . . the A . . . A . . . A . . . Acorn Field. You, you know it, don't you?

Wife: Yes . . .

Husband: When I finish the so . . . so . . . so . . . sowing in the spring, I am thinking of clearing pa . . . pa . . . part of that field.

Wife: Clearing that field?

Husband: Ŭng.

Wife: How . . . can you . . . possibly . . . clear that field?

Husband: I e . . . examined the area ca . . . ca . . . ca . . . carefully last summer. I know it will take a lot of e . . . energy, ...

Wife: Yes. . . if you. . . work hard. . . . But it is a steep area. And the field is covered with rocks. . . .

Husband: Tha. . . that is the reason why it still r. . . re. . . remains uncultivated.

Wife: Well, that. . . that is true.

Husband: If I could plant sweet potatoes the. . . there, it would help us in so. . . so. . . solving the f. . . f. . . food problem a bit.

Wife: Then do you think that we can. . . have all of the harvest?

Husband: Although we would have to g. . . give some of it to the go. . . government as tax, there would still be a li. . . li. . . little left over for us.

Wife: I too,. . . after the child is born,. . . will come up there and help you.

Husband: If tha. . . that happens, we may be able to p. . . plant something else the following s. . . spring.

Wife: As long as. . . a severe famine year,. . . like two years ago. . . doesn't happen again,. . . .

Husband: Well, . . . bu. . . but I. . . I am. . . .

Wife: . . .? . . .

Husband: But.

Wife: But what. . .?

Husband: The. . . the thi. . . thi. . . thieves. I have heard that there are many thi. . . thieves.

Wife: Although there are many thieves,. . . what can they possibly steal. . . from us?

Husband: I. . . I . . . I don't mean. . . .

Wife: . . . .?

Husband: Why should we wo. . . wo. . . wo. . . worry about the thi. . . thieves? Bu. . . bu. . . but. . . *(The Wife nods at though she understands what he means.)* If famine years continue, there will be more thi. . . thi. . . thi. . . thieves and robbers. Then there will be p. . . p. . . p. . . punitive expeditions.

Wife: Yōbo. *(She holds her husband's arm.)*

Husband: If I was to be d. . . d. . . drafted as a so. . . so. . . so. . . soldier,. . . .

Wife: There are. . . so many. . . policemen. . . in the government. Then. . . .

Husband: There are ma. . . ma. . . many soldiers to watch u. . . u. . . u. . . us. But they ca. . . ca. . . can't match the gangs of thieves and robbers. Don't you remember even the so. . . so. . . soldiers from Se. . . Seoul were all ki. . . ki. . . killed a few years ago?

Wife: Aigo.

Husband: . . .

Wife: Well, *yŏbo*. . . what. . . is the recent news?

Husband: Do you mean about the thi. . . thi. . . thi. . . thieves?

Wife: Yes.

Husband: Ŭng I think they ra. . . ra. . . ra. . . ran away to Manchuria.

Wife: Is that right?

Husband: They sa. . . sa. . . sa. . . sa. . . sa. . . sa. . . said so.

Wife: For heaven's sake, I hope so. The year of abundance will continue . . . from the time when our baby will be born. . . . Then there will be no more thieves. . . .

Husband: Tha. . . tha. . . tha. . . that is right.

Wife: Really. . . that is right.

Husband: I wish tha. . . tha. . . tha. . . that would happen. *(As he caresses his wife's abdomen.)* The ha. . . ha. . . happy baby. . . . It will make our lives ea. . . ea. . . easy.

Wife: Yŏbo. *(She caresses her abdomen.)* I think it will be a happy baby.

Husband: Well, how do you know?

Wife: Why shouldn't I know? Look at these. *(As she touches the grain sacks.)* That lord. . . has loaned. . . these to us. . . again.

Husband: Re. . . re. . . really. Mr. Ki. . . Ki. . . Ki. . . Kim from the other vi. . . village had to return home with an e. . . empty hand. The rich lord would loan him nothing.

Wife: See. Everything is due to our. . . happy. . . baby. *(She touches the grain sacks as though caressing them.)* Look. The baby has brought us a lot of seed grain.

Husband: A lo. . . lo. . . lo. . . lot. *(He absently picks up the grain sacks and moves them a little. Now she presses them* down.)

Wife: In addition,. . . . *(She listens to some sounds. The Husband does the same.)* The snow has. . . . *(The Husband nods. She holds his arm. The Husband caresses his wife's abdomen. She smiles. Now she gathers the millet in the sack and then presses them into order. The Husband does the same as though helping her.)*

Husband: If it is a bo. . . bo. . . boy. . . .

Wife: He will help. . . papa.

Husband: He will wo. . . wo. . . wo. . . wo. . . work in the f. . . f. . . f. . . field.

Wife: If it is a girl. . . .

Husband: She will help ma. . . ma. . . ma. . . ma. . . mama and run the ho. . . ho. . . house.

Wife: Yōbo.

Husband: Ŭng?

Wife: If I. . . want to. . . go to. . . to field?

Husband: I will t. . . t. . . t. . . *(A pause)* t. . . t. . . take you.

Wife: Really? That is good.

Husband: Tha. . . tha. . . tha. . . that is right.

Wife: I will put. . . the baby. . . in the cool. . . shade.

Husband: Ŭng.

Wife: The baby will see. . . the squirrels. . . and will listen. . . to the birds.

Husband: We will also give the baby a ba. . . ba. . . ba. . . bath in the s. . . s. . . s. . . stream.

Wife: When the clouds. . . travel in the sky. . . over the baby. . . it will. . . smile at them.

Husband: As long as a year of abundance arrives. . . .

Wife: As long as. . . there are no thieves. . . .

Husband: We are t. . . talking about the sa. . . same thing.

Wife: Really. That is right.

Husband: . . . *(The couple smile at each other.)*

Husband: Yō. . . yō. . . yō. . . yō. . . yōbo. Let's go to be. . . be. . . be. . . bed.

Wife: Well,. . . let's sleep.

Husband:. . .
(*The couple smile. The Wife extinguishes the oil lamp. The howling sounds of wolves in the distance.*)

ACT II

Spring. The same place. The crying sound of a baby. The wife comes out of the kitchen and enters the room. She is carrying the baby in her arms.

Wife: It is all right. . . . It is all right. Our baby. . . he is hungry. . . . Here it is. . . . (*She begins to nurse the baby. The baby still cries.*) No milk. . . . What shall I do? . . . . There is nothing for Mama to eat. . . so there is no milk (*She cuddles the baby. She goes back to the room and leaves the baby there to sleep. She returns. A Neighbor Woman from the other side of the village, Kaettong's mother, enters.*)
Woman: Is. . . the baby. . . growing well?
Wife: Oh, Kaettong's mother.
Woman: He must be sleeping.
Wife: Yes, . . . only a few moments ago. . . .
Woman: Does he have. . . enough milk to drink?
Wife: So so.
Woman: (*She clicks her tongue.*) How can he have enough milk. . . since you don't have anything to eat? Even a healthy person is hungry and weak. . . this spring. You must have a craving. . . for all sorts of food. Take. . . this.
Wife: Oh, my,. . . . What is this?
Woman: What do you expect from me? This is nothing but acorn jello.
Wife: You also have many children. . . at home.
Woman: Since there are nine hungry mouths, as little as this doesn't help them much. So I brought it to the person who

ought to eat it.

Wife: You also must be. . . short of food.

Woman: When I was suffering from typhoid fever last summer, . . . who would have helped me. . . if it wasn't you? I must thank you. . . . I won't forget that.

Wife: But. . . .

Woman: You must taste it. . . .Here. . . . I also brought some soy sauce for you. *(She hands the Wife a small earthern jar.)*

Wife: Oh my goodness, . . . I am so indebted to you.

Woman: Well, bring out a plate.

(The Wife goes to the kitchen and returns with two plates and spoons.)

Woman: That is good. *(She takes some acorn jello from the large scooped wooden bowl and gives it to the Wife.)*

Wife: You, too, elder sister.

Woman: (As she waves her hand.) No, I didn't come here to eat. Well, . . . eat it. *(The Wife eats a spoonful of acorn jello.)* How does it taste?

Wife: As sweet as honey. . . honey.

Woman: (As she raises her shoulders in pride.) I know at least how to make acorn jello. *(She watches the Wife who eats the acorn jello.)* Aigu.*. . . You have a swollen face. Had your mother seen you in this situation, she would have felt such agony deep in her heart. *(She wipes her tears with her skirt belt. The Wife stops eating and weeps.)* Aigo. This, this silly chatterbox mouth. *(She slaps her mouth.)* I deserve harsh treatment. . . by my husband. Well, . . . my husband says. . . if my mouth and my stomach *(As she points)* had been shut, . . . the gate to his fortune would have been wide open. But to tell you the truth, . . . do you know who makes my stomach keep opening? . . . You know him, don't you?

Wife: (She laughs.) Although you have. . . many children, . . . when they grow up. . . I suppose. . . they can make their

---

* *Aigu:* a synonym for *aigo*

own living.

Woman: Make their own living? . . . . What do you mean by that? Where is the land to make their living? . . . . From where can they get their food? . . . . By the way, have you heard. . . about the story?

Wife: Excuse me?

Woman: Really. Never in my life have I heard such a strange story. When the world gets ugly, . . . there come to pass. . . so many strange things. Have you not heard the neighing sound of a dragon-horse?*

Wife: (She shakes her head.)

Woman: I have not heard it either. . . but I am told that Soettŏl's father who lives on the other side of the hill. . . has heard it twice.

Wife: Is that right?

Woman: Ŭng.

Wife: How. . . does it neigh?

Woman: I don't know since I have never heard it. Even last night, . . . I tried to listen for the sound, . . . but my husband didn't let me alone. After a long day's hard work in the field with a hoe, . . . I tried to rest. But my husband, as usual, jumped and bounced on me in the night. . . . So last night I had to work as hard as I did in the field during the day. Afterwards, I was as dead as a log until the dawn. So. . . how could I possibly hear the neighing sound of the dragon-horse? I don't have an extra ear for that. I guess I am now getting old. So I can't help it. . . It is said that. . . if a superman were born, . . . the birth of a dragon-horse would also follow his birth.

Wife: A superman.

Woman: (As she nods.) That is right. He is an absolute being who may bring us abundant food. . . drink. . . and protection.

Wife: A superman? . . . . What would he look like?

---

* dragon-horse: a swift horse

Woman: Well, once a long time ago. . . my deceased grandmother told me. . . a superman was born with scales over
his skin. . . and wings. . . under his arms.

Wife: Aigo. . . . If he is like that, . . . then our baby. . . is not
a superman.

Woman: Of course, . . . I hope he is not one. In addition, she
told me that a superman could walk a moment after his
birth.

Wife: Our baby. . . cannot even roll over yet by himself. Ha,
ha! Then I don't think he is a superman.

Woman: Of course, he is not. If he were a superman, the
officials would not only kill him but also put his parents to
death. . . . Furthermore, they would turn the whole village
into a waste land.

Wife: Why. . . do that to the village?

Woman: A long time ago, . . . a superman was born. . . in a
village. So the officials burnt down the whole village, . . .
saying that an inauspicious sign had fallen upon the village.

Wife: Aigo. . . . If that happens, what shall we do? Our innocent baby will. . . . *(She looks toward the room.)*

Woman: Now, . . . the mountain from which the neighing
sound of a dragon-horse is supposedly heard. . . is not
located near our village. Since it rather belongs to the other
new village, . . . perhaps a superman has been born in that
village.

Wife: Well, for heaven's sake, . . . I hope so.

Woman: I have heard that the officials believe. . . that a
superman must have been born in that village, . . . because
a dragon-horse has been neighing in that mountain. I am
also told that. . . they have been examining every child
under the age of ten, . . . including the babies. If a child of
distinction is found, he is instantly arrested and sent to the
government.

Wife: Aigo.

Woman: All parents are afraid to have their children look
strong these days. . . well, . . . since then. . . all my

children. . . have been doing nothing but lying by the
fire. . . telling me that they can no longer go to the
mountains to cut wood. They simply refuse to carry. . . so
much as a chamber pot. . . within a distance of a couple
of feet.

Wife: Oh my goodness.

Woman: Well, don't you think. . . all of them will be spoiled?
Under the present situation, . . . since they don't want to
be supermen, all of them have become living corpses. . . .

Wife: Do you mean that not only the babies, . . . well, . . . but
also the grown up children. . . ?

Woman: Well, . . . because no one knows how old the dragon-
horse is, . . . they also don't know how old the child is
who rides on it. No one. . . has seen the dragon-horse. So
. . . the officials are. . . blindly checking all children who
are not yet married.

Wife: (As though she is relived.) Well, I thought. . . .

Woman: Aigo. . . . Now. . . I must go home. Well, . . .
shall we see the baby? Wait a minute. . . . Let me see
him. *(While still sitting she leans over and opens the door
quietly. Then she looks at the baby while half-lying on the
doorsill. She stands up.)* He is handsome. Like a superman.
Don't you think?

Wife: (Happily) I think so.

(The Husband enters in haste.)

Husband: Yŏ. . . yŏ. . . yŏ. . . yŏ. . . yŏbo.

Woman: Why are you so short of breath?

Husband: Ah, ah, ah. W. . . well, ju. . . ju. . . ju. . . just now
the po. . . police force. . . mar. . . marched into the mo. . .
mo. . . mountain th. . . through the A. . . A. . . A. . . Acorn
Valley. Ju. . . ju. . . ju. . . just now.

Woman: The police. . . ? Why?

Husband: They said they were go. . . go. . . going to capture
the d. . . d. . . dragon-horse.

Woman: Is the dragon-horse. . . in our village?

Husband: It was or. . . or. . . or. . . order from the mayor. It

seems to me the police have begun to sea. . . search every vi
. . . village.

Woman: I hope. . . neither the superman. . . nor the dragon-
horse. . . will be found in our village.

Husband: Since the b. . . b. . . b. . . blood-thirsty police force
climbed the mountain, they might capture the d. . .
dragon-horse or. . . .

Woman: Do you think. . . the dragon-horse. . . will be caught
easily?

Wife: Oh, look. You are. . . sweating.

Husband: I. . . I also f. . . f. . . followed them to the f. . . foot
of the mountain.

Wife: Why did you have to follow them?

Husband: W. . . w. . . well. It appeared that they were going
to sea. . . search the mo. . . mo. . . mo. . . mountain for a
f. . . few days. When I was ploughing in the lower field,
the o. . . officers came. They forced me to carry a lot of
w. . . wine and food to the A. . . A. . . Acorn Field. Then
they le. . . let me go. So I came back.

Woman: Why didn't they carry. . . their own food. . . on their
backs?. . . Did they think that. . . they would be struck to
death by lightning. . . if they happend to carry their own
food? If they hadn't found you in the field, . . . would they
have had to throw away their food?

Husband: Oh, no. Someone would have been found to carry
their f. . . food up there.

Woman: I suppose so. I know the officers would not carry
their own food. We haven't even finished. . . the sowing
yet. . . .In this busy season. . . .Ha, ha! Indeed, the
dragon-horse wouldn't have to neigh for nothing. . . .
There must be a reason for neighing. . . . Well, who
carried the wine and food?

Husband: W. . . w. . . w. . . well. It was you. . . you. . .
your children's father.

Woman: *Aigu.* Oh, dear. He must have been caught by them
. . . while he was working near the roadside. Imagine. He

ploughed. . . even last night, too.

Husband: In the n. . . n. . . n. . . night, too?

   (The Wife turns her face away awkwardly.)

Woman: Oh, no. I didn't mean the real field. . . *Aigu.* My
chatterbox mouth. *(She slaps her mouth.)*

   (At this time the sound of singing is heard.)

> *Our baby, a good baby*
> *The baby which grows without milk.*
> *The baby which grows while fussing.*
> *If a lean year arrives, he becomes a thief.*
>
> *If he becomes a thief, there wouldn't be a place*
> *For him to come and go even in this wide world.*
> *His chopped head will be hung high*
> *On the pillar of the government building.*

   *(The singing is now heard nearer. It is a hoarse voice. The
three people on the stage direct their ears in the direction
from which the singing is heard. The Husband moves a
few steps toward the sound. An old woman enters. Her
hair is all grey. Her back is bent. She wears a ragged
costume. She carries a cane in her hand. Like many
Korean ladies of ancient times, a small bundle is attached
to her waist. It is flat and empty.)*

Husband: From wh. . . wh. . . wh. . . where. . . .

Old Woman: *(She stares at the people.)*

Woman: She is a stranger.

Old Woman: Give me some water.

   *(The Wife exits into the kitchen. The Old Woman sits on
the ground.)*

Wife: *(She enters.)* Here it is.

Old Woman: *(She takes the bowl and drinks the water from
it.)*

Woman: Where have you come from?

Old Woman: From there. *(She raises her arm to indicate that
she has traveled a long distance.)*

Woman: From there? From the other side of the mountain? *(The Old Woman nods.)* Where are you going?

Old Woman: I am going to get my son.

Woman: Your son?

Old Woman: My son.

Woman: Where is your son?

Old Woman: In the government building.

Woman: In the government building? *(The Old Woman nods.)* Where in the government building?

Old Woman: In a high place.

Woman: (Confused) Well, why has a person who is in such a high position left his mother in the street?. How high a position is he in?

Old Woman: A high place.

Woman: Possibly, his position may not be as high as that of the mayor.

Old Woman: Higher than his place.

Woman: Well, did you say that his place is higher than that of the mayor?

Old Woman: A higher place.

Woman: Excuse me? What kind of position is that?

Old Woman: On top of the pillar.

(The three people look at each other.)

Woman: Then. . . is your son possibly the thief? *(The Old Woman nods.)* Is your son the thief whose head is hung on the pillar of the government building? *(The Old Woman nods. The three people retreat a few steps from her.)*

Old Woman: Even though it is only his head, I must get it and bury it. Thank you for the water. *(She stands up with the support of her cane. She moves in the opposite direction from which she entered. She sing.)*

If he becomes a thief, there wouldn't be a place
For him to come and go even in this wide world.
His chopped head will be hung high
On the pillar of the government building.

When a black magpie pecks,
Papa, mama, and my papa
Will bewail their fortune in life.
I'm afraid of having another baby.
Our baby. It is no longer ours.

(The other people on stage remain still until the Old Woman has walked away.)

Woman: Well, then, where is. . . my husband. . . now?
Husband: He is s. . . s. . . still on the mo. . . mo. . . mountain.
Woman: With the officers?
Husband: Yes.
Woman: I must be going since I left only the living corpses at home. . . . The house must look like a waste land. . . whether it is a superman or a dragon-horse,. . . it is an enemy to us. . . an enemy. *(She exits hastily.)*
(The crying sound of the baby. The Wife comes out with the baby in her arms. As she thinks about something, she sings.)

Wife: *Our baby, a good baby.*
Our baby which grows without milk.
The baby which grows while fussing.
If a lean year arrives, he becomes a thief.

(Night of the same day. The Husband and the Wife are sitting facing each other. The baby sleeps nearby. The grain sacks still remain in the room. The sound of the wind. They direct their ears in the direction from which the sound is heard.)

Wife: Do you think he will be caught?
Husband: W. . . w. . . well, I am not certain.
(The howling sounds of wolves.)

ACT III

The same place. The Wife and the Neighbor Woman enter. They carry hoes.

Wife: I wonder whether he is awake. *(To the Woman)* I am. . . just returning home. . . from the field. *(She walks into the room and comes out with the baby in her arms. She sits down on the ground and nurses the baby.)*

Woman: (As she looks over at the baby.) What a docile baby. . . *(She sits down in the fashion of half lying on the ground.) Aigu.* We never had a year. . . without calamities and misfortunes. Since we had plenty of snow last winter, . . . I thought we would have a year of abundance. . . but. . . unexpectedly, we are now troubled by the dragon-horse. Every man in the village. . . is on the mountain, . . . searching for the dragon-horse. Now I wonder when they are going to come home to plough the field. . . and sow the seeds. In addition, . . . for the past ten days. . . the officers have been taking our food, chickens, and even acorn jello. They might just make the villagers starve to death. . . before they catch the dragon-horse.

Wife: How about your chicken. . .?

Woman: Which chicken do you mean?

Wife: I mean the rooster.

Woman: Well, . . . which rooster do you mean?

Wife: Did you have. . . more than one rooster?

Woman: Do you mean the bird rooster, . . . or the human rooster? Which rooster do you mean?

Wife: Aigu. You,. . . what are you talking about?

Woman: The bird rooster has been gone for three days. . . and the human rooster. . . is still on the mountain.

Wife: My baby's father. . . came home yesterday. . . for a short time.

Woman: What did he have to say? Are they going to stay there. . . until summer? Or are they trying to conceive a dragon-horse in their own stomach?

Wife: He said they might come home. . . today.

Woman: Is that right? Do you mean they can come home without capturing the dragon-horse?

Wife: As you have heard, it is impossible to catch it.

Woman: That is what I have heard. When they hear the neighing sound of the dragon-horse in this direction and they come here,. . . they now hear it in that direction. So they feel like they are bewitched. . . by the neighing sound of the dragon-horse. I wonder why it had to happen? Whosoever fault it is,. . . the officers are taking their anger out on the villagers. Besides they have been devouring. . . our chickens, cakes, and wine. . . both day and night. . . . Especially, at night. . . when they hear the neighing sound of the dragon-horse, they simply order out husbands to go and search for it while they sit in their rooms.

Wife: What shall we do?

Woman: Anyway, . . . well, . . . I am worried about this year's farming. . . . Aren't you also worried about it. . . ? I wonder when I can sow the seeds?

Wife: I am told that they might come. . . today.

Woman: Well,. . . . that is right, isn't it?

Wife: Yes.

Woman: The officers are just giving the innocent farmers a hard time. . . without accomplishing anything. Well, . . . the dragon-horse is a sacred thing, isn't it? If so, . . . how can it possibly be caught. . . by human hands?

Wife: I think it is.

Woman: Of course, it is a sacred thing. This is a horse which is supposedly born to carry a superman. . . . If so, how can it be caught by a simple man. . . like my husband? The only horse that is easy enough for him to ride in this whole wide world. . . is none other than. . . this woman. *(The Wife pretends she does not understand what has been said. The Wife stands up and takes the baby into the room and lets him sleep there. Now she returns.)* What a docile baby. . . such a docile baby. . . well, . . . I must go. . . and plough a

little more. . . before the sunset. *Aigu.* Even though he
gives me a bit of a rough time at night, . . . I hope my husband will come home soon. If any man who carries a bit of
wood on his back or a hoe in his hand can be called a superman, . . . then every man in the village could be one. Since
none of our children wants to work under the present con-
ditions, . . . I now have to do everything by myself. . .
ploughing. . . wood cutting, . . . and cooking. *(The two
women take up their hoes and begin to walk out.)*
Wife: (As she points at something in the distance) Look!
Woman: Well, they are finally coming down.
Wife: Yes, the officers are walking. . . along the stream.
Woman: They are not heading toward town. I wonder. . .
why they are coming. . . in this direction?
Wife: Really. . . that is right.
Woman: Look at them!
Wife: Yes?
Woman: It looks like. . . they are going to take a rest.
Wife: Yes, . . . I think so.
Woman: I must go. *(She exits in haste.)*
*Wife: (She follows the Neighbor Woman a couple of steps.
Then she turns around. The sound of someone walking is
heard from the room.)* Is he awake? *(She goes to the door
and opens it.)* Aigumŏni! Oh my! *(She falls down with a
thud. She looks into the room trembling with fear. The
baby who is walking around the room is seen through the
door. [It is a doll.] He walks carefully while flapping his
arms up and down.)* Aigu. What shall I do? *Aigu.* What
shall I do? *(She crawls to the door and sits by the doorsill as
she leans against it.)* Aigu. My baby. *Aigu.* My baby.
Baby: (From the loud speaker, an echo-like voice is heard.) I
can no longer endure this.
Wife: No. My baby. You can't do that.
*(A red flood light upon the Wife. She struggles like a mute
as she moves her arms and legs up and down in all directions while she is half sitting and half lying. The baby*

keeps walking around in the room. She crawls to the door
and shuts it. Then she turns the latch in the door. She
listens to something as she did while she was waiting for
her husband's return in Act I. But her present mood is
totally different from the previous one. The sound of
someone approaching. She directs her ear in the direction
from which the sound is heard. She repeats this action
several times. She walks to the gate and looks into the
distance. The Husband enters. He walks slowly. He is
tired. He drops the net bag from his back. Then he plops
down with a thud.)

Husband: Aigu.

Wife: . . .

Husband: It was a f. . . fruitless labor.

Wife: . . .

Husband: I have heard that the ma. . . ma. . . mayor is in a
wild ra. . . ra. . . rage.

Wife: . . .

Husband: The o. . . officers became very s. . . s. . . spiteful,
too.

Wife: . . .

Husband: I am told that the ma. . . ma. . . mayor told the
o. . . o. . . officers that they won't be allowed to return to
the to. . . to. . . town unless they catch the ho. . . ho. . .
horse.

Wife: . . .

Husband: W. . . well. They said they were going to ca. . .
camp out by the s. . . s. . . stream for the n. . . n. . . night to
se. . . se. . . search every house for the su . . . su . . .
superman tomorrow. Ah. . . Ah. . . Aigu. My, my fate!

Wife: . . .

Husband: (He stares at his wife.)

Wife: (She looks at her husband.)

Husband: Wha. . . wha. . . what is the matter?

Wife: (She looks down at her husband's net bag on the ground.)

Husband: Ŭng?

Wife: (She looks at her husband.)

Husband: Why are you just lo. . . lo. . . looking at me like that?

Wife: (She shakes her head.)

Husband: (He holds his wife's arm. He suddenly looks in all directions. He does not find anything unusual.)

Wife: (She looks at the room. The door is tightly shut.)
    (The sound of someone walking is heard from the room.)

Husband: (He looks at the room.) What is that? What is that? *(He walks towards the room.)*

Wife: (She stops him.)

Husband: (As though he is beginning to sense that something unusual has happened.) Ŭng?

Wife: (She lets her husband's arm slip from her hand.) Yŏbo.

Husband: . . .

Wife: Yŏbo. We are in big trouble.

Husband: Wha. . . what? *(As if he is beginning to comprehend the meaning of his wife's talk, he stops going toward the room.)* Is it t. . . t. . . t. . . t. . . true?

Wife: (She nods.)

Husband: (He stares at the room. The sound of someone walking is heard from the room. He looks at his wife. The Wife nods. The sound of the doorknob being pulled by the baby is heard.) Aigu. *(He plops down with a thud. The Wife crouches down near her husband. They stare at each other. Now they look in the direction of the room.)* Yŏ. . . yŏ. . . yŏ. . . yŏbo. *(He stands up and walks towards the room. He looks back at his wife. The Wife stands near her husband. She goes to the door and tries to unlock the latch. But she stops suddenly. She now peeps into the room through a hole in the paper of the door. She moves away from the door so that her husband can peep into the room. The Husband peeps into the room through the hole.)* Aigu. *(He plops down with a thud. He crawls backward to the middle of the yard. The Wife keeps standing by the door. In a low voice.)* Yŏ. . . yŏ. . . yŏ. . . yŏbo. What, what. . . shall. . . we do? *(The Wife keeps standing by the door. He waves his hand signaling his wife to come to him. She still stands. He again waves his hand to his wife. The Wife walks into the yard. She crouches near her husband.)* Wha. . . wha. . . wha. . . what shall we do? *(The Wife looks at him as though she can no longer hear anything he is saying.)* Wha. . . wha. . . wha. . . what shall we do?

Wife: (The couple sit down facing each other. A long pause. The sound of someone approaching. They direct their ears in the direction from which the sound is heard. The sound of the wind.)

Husband: It is the sound of the w. . . w. . . wind.

(The Wife stands up and walks into the kitchen. She returns with a wicker basketful of herbs. She takes the herbs out of the basket and puts them in front of the door. Then she sits down as if to block the door. The Husband is watching carefully what his wife does. As though he does not understand the meaning of his wife's action, he shakes his head lightly. Then he glances at the house gate. The rattling sounds of the doorknob.)

Wife: (She sings slowly in an ordinary lullaby tone.)

Our baby, a good baby.
The baby which grows without milk.
If a lean year arrives, he becomes a thief.

If he becomes a thief, there wouldn't be a place
For him to come and go in this wide world.
His chopped head will be hung high
On the pillar of the government building.

When a black magpie pecks,
Papa, mama, and my papa
Will bewail their fortune in life.
I'm afraid of having another baby.
Our baby. It is no longer ours.

(The rattling sound of the doorknob. The sound stops sud-

denly. The Husband looks at his wife. Then he glances in the direction where the house gate stands. The Wife browses through the herbs. The couple direct their ears in the direction from which the sound of the wind is heard.)

Husband: It is the sound of the w. . . w. . . w. . . wind.

(The sound of the wind. The Wife again browses through the herbs. The Husband's eyes follow the motions of the Wife's hands.

The Wife stands up and walks into the kitchen. The Husband looks at the Wife's back. The Wife returns. The Husband looks at the Wife until she sits in front of the door and browses through the herbs. He glances at the gate. He watches his wife. He straightens up lightly as though he has a question to ask his wife. But he stops. He stands up and walks to the backyard. He returns with a bundle of straws. The Wife looks at him. The Husband puts the straws near the gate and begins to make a straw rope. A long pause.

The Husband suddenly stops making the straw rope. The Wife also stops browsing through the herbs. The sound of someone approaching is heard from the outside. A pause.

The Husband walks to the gate reluctantly. Then he directs his ears to the outside. The sound of someone approaching. He returns holding his breath.)

Husband: *(As he looks at his wife)* It is a s. . . s. . . s. . . squirrel.

(The Wife drops her head. She begins to browse through the herbs. The Husband begins to make the straw rope. He stops and looks at his wife who keeps browsing through the herbs.

Suddenly. The chirping sounds of birds. The frightened couple lift their heads and look at each other. Then they glance at the door.

The Wife again browses through the herbs, while the Husband begins to make the straw rope. A pause.

   The stage gets dark suddenly. The couple look at the
sky.)
Husband: It is a c. . . c . . . c. . . c . . . cloud.
   (The stage light returns slowly. The rattling sound of the
   doorknob. The Husband jumps up and plugs his ears with
   fingers. He looks at the door and drops hands from his
   ears. As though he is confused, he looks at the gate. Now
   he turns around and looks at his wife.)
Wife: *(She sings slowly in a sad tone.)*

   Our baby, a docile baby.
   Our baby which grows without milk.
   If a lean year arrives, he becomes a thief.

   If he becomes a thief, there wouldn't be a place
   For him to come and go in this wide world.
   His chopped head will be hung high
   On the pillar of the government building.

   When a black magpie pecks,
   Papa, mama, and my papa
   Will bewail their fortune in life.
   I'm afraid of having another baby.
   Our baby. It is no longer ours.

   (The rattling sounds of the doorknob. The sounds stop
   suddenly. Meanwhile, the Husband, who has been keep-
   ing his eyes on the situation outside the gate, returns. The
   Wife browses casually through the herbs. The Husband
   sits down and begins to make the straw rope. It seems as if
   he is making the straw rope by twisting the agony in his
   heart. The evening glow in the sky. It is beginning to get.
   dark. Now the glow changes into a crimson color. Then it
   changes to purple. A blackout. A pause. The neighing
   sound of a horse in the distance. The frightened couple
   freeze. A flood light on the Husband's face. Another flood
   light on the Wife's face. The rattling sounds of the door-
   knob.)

Baby: (From the loud speakers. In an echolike tone) I am
hungry.
   *(The Wife and the Husband stand up one by one. The
   Wife walks into the room. A blackout. A pause. A light in
   the room comes up. The Wife walks out of the room. A
   flood light on her face. Another flood light on the Husband's face. The couple walk toward the middle of the
   yard and fall down. A pause. The sound of an owl
   hooting. The couple direct their ears in the direction from
   which the owl hoots are heard. The sound of someone approaching. The flood lights dim out. The stage is dark
   again. A pause. A flood light on the Husband's face.)*
Husband: A b. . . b. . . b. . . bird is f. . . f. . . flying over us.
   *(A flood light on the Wife's face. The flapping sounds of a
   bird's wings. The bird is flying from one branch to
   another. The sounds of owls hooting.*

   *The stage is dark. A pause. The howling sounds of
   wolves. At last, the lights on the stage return slowly. The
   flood lights on the faces of the crouching couple. They
   turn their heads towards the room. Suddenly, the shadow
   of the baby who is pulling the doorknob on the paper of
   the door. The rattling sounds of the doorknob. The
   sounds get louder.*

   *The Husband turns his face toward his wife. A flood
   light on his face.)*
Wife: (She sings slowly in a sad tone.)

Our baby, a docile baby.
Our baby which grows without milk.
If a lean year arrives, he becomes a thief.

If he becomes a thief, there wouldn't be a place
For him to come and go in this wide world.
His chopped head will be hung high
On the pillar of the government building.

When a black magpie pecks,
Papa, mama, and my papa

Will bewail their fortune in life.
I'm afraid of having another baby.
Our baby. It is no longer ours.

(A Pause. The rattling sounds of the doorknob stops. The
neighing sound of a horse. The louder rattling sounds of
the doorknob. The baby's voice from the speakers: "My
horse!")
Husband: *(As he suddenly stands up) Yŏ. . . yŏbo. (He looks*
down at his wife.)
Wife: *(As she looks at him) No! (She holds onto her husband's*
trousers.)
(The Husband looks around in the darkness. At this mo-
ment, the baby's voice from the speakers: "My horse!"
The rattling sounds of the doorknob. The Husband
kicks his wife and strides towards the door. The Wife
follows him and holds onto his leg. He kicks her hard. The
Wife falls down.
The Husband unlatches the door and walks into the
room. The shadow of a man on the paper of the door. The
large shadow knocks down the shadow of the baby. The
shadow which indicates that a seed grain sack is being
placed on the baby appears on the paper of the door.
The Husband walks out of the room. The Wife sudden-
ly stands up. The Husband crouches down on the ground
as he holds down his wife who struggles to escape from his
arms.
The shadow of the struggling baby under the grain sack
on the paper of the door. A long pause. From the room,
an echolike sound: "Mama!"
The Wife stands up. The Husband kicks her as hard as
he did before and walks into the room. The shadow of
another seed grain sack being placed on the baby by the
Husband on the paper of the door.
The Husband walks out of the room. He crouches
down on the ground, holding his wife as he did before.

*Once in a while, he lifts his head and looks at the shadow
on the paper of the door. Finally, the shadow of the baby
stops moving. The sad echolike neighing sound of a
horse.*

*The oil lamp in the room dims out. The moonlight.
The moonlight dims down gradually. The clouds cover the
moon. The sound of the wind. The stage is dark. The
faint moonlight.*

*The Husband walks out carrying something on his
A-frame carrier on his back. The sound of the gusting
sound.)*

ACT IV

Dawn. The next day. The chirping sounds of birds. The
stage is empty. The door to the room is shut. The faint singing
sound is heard in the distance.

*Our baby, a docile baby.
Our baby which grows without milk.
If a lean year arrives, he becomes a thief.*

*(The singing sound gradually becomes louder. It is a
hoarse voice. But her singing tone is clear. The Old
Woman enters. She is in the same ragged costume as she
was in Act II. However, the bundle on her waist is swelled.
The bundle looks as if it holds a gourd. The Wife enters
from the backyard. She stares at the Old Woman.)*
Old Woman: I found him. *(She bring her bundle around to
the front.)* I found my child.
Wife: *(She stares at the round bundle.)*
Old Woman: *(As she caresses the bundle.)* I found my child.
*(The Wife walks to the back of the house. The Old
Woman sits on the ground. She begins to sing a lullaby in*

*a mumbling tone while she caresses the bundle. She is
almost inaudible. Once in a while, her tone gets high, giving an impression that she is still singing. The Wife
returns absent-mindedly. She hands the Old Woman a
bowl of water.)*
Old Woman: Thank you. *(She drinks the water.)* Thank you.
*(She puts the bowl on the ground. Then she adjusts the
bundle back to her waist.)* You are my truly docile child
who no longer feels cold, hot, thirsty, hungry, or fussy.
*(She stands up. The Wife looks at the Old Woman's bun-
dle.)* Let's go to the sunny place where the birds sing. I will
bury you near the field where I do weeding. Let's go. *(She
begins to walk as she cradles the bundle on her waist with
one hand.)* It is quite light. It is lighter than he was in jail.
(She exits.)
   *(The Wife stands still as she sees the Old Woman off. She
   looks in the direction in which the Old Woman has gone.
   The chirping sounds of birds. It is a bright spring day. She
   keeps standing as she directs her ear in the direction from
   which the chirping sounds of birds are heard. She walks
   into the room.*
      *A pause. The Husband enters carrying his A-frame on
   his back and a hoe in his hand. He puts the A-frame on
   the ground without a word. He stands still.)*
Husband: *(Faintly)* Yŏ. . . yŏ. . . yŏ. . . yŏbo.
   *(The Husband walks to the backyard. He returns. He
   exits through the gate as he looks in all directions. A few
   seconds later, he returns. He plops down on the ground
   with a thud and drops his head. A pause. Suddenly, he
   looks at the door to the room. He opens it. The Wife
   whose body is hanging on the girdle is seen. [It is a doll.]
   He runs into the room and takes her body down.)*
Husband: Yŏ. . . yŏ. . . yŏ. . . yŏ. . . yŏbo.
   *(The Husband holds the Wife's body and shakes it. He
   crouches down near his wife's body. His head sinks between his knees. A pause. He stands up. He puts the belt,*

which was used by his wife for the hanging, on the girdle.
The neighing sound of a horse. A baby on dragon-horse's
back [both the baby and the dragon-horse are dolls.]
enters through the gate. A flood light on the Wife's body.
The Husband walks down to the yard. As soon as he sees
the baby on the horseback, he crouches down on the
ground.)

Husband: I have just re. . . re. . . returned home after bu. . .
bu. . . bu. . . bu. . . burying you.

(The baby shakes his head and gives a bouquet of azalea
to his father. The Husband walks to the baby as though
he is in dream and takes bouquet.)

Baby: *(From the loud speakers)* Mama, mama!

Husband: *(He enters into the room and puts the bouquet on*
the chest of the Wife's body.) Yŏ. . . yŏ. . . yŏ. . . yōbo. . . .
You. . . you. . . you. . . your ba. . . ba. . . ba. . . baby has
brought the bouquet. He has returned a. . . a. . . a. . .
alive.

(The Wife [a doll] takes the bouquet and stands up. She
walks to the yard and embraces the baby.)

Baby: *(From the loud speaker)* Mama and papa. Please get on
the dragon-horse's back quickly.

Husband: *(He helps his wife get on the dragon-horse's back.)*
Please g. . . g. . . g. . . go qu. . . qu. . . qu. . . . . .
qu. . . qu. . . quickly. The pe. . . pe. . . pe. . . people
will co. . . co. . . co. . . come. I to. . . to. . . to. . . told
them that you were de. . . de. . . de. . . dead. The vi. . .
vi. . . vi. . . villagers will co. . . co. . . co. . . . . .co. . .
co. . . co. . . come. *(The baby waves his hand.)*

Wife: Quick! Quick! The police are coming.

Husband: *(As he wipes away the tears with his sleeve)* W. . .
w. . . w. . . well. *(He does not get on the dragon-horse's*
back. He now holds the rein and leads the dragon-horse
through the gate.)

(The empty stage. A blackout. The empty stage becomes
bright again. A few villagers and several policemen

enter.)
Villager I: Look!
Policeman I: *(As he abruptly pulls the doorknob)* Where did they go?
Policeman II: Is this possible?
Villager II: Maybe, during the night. . . .
Policeman III: Hŭm.
Villager I: I was told that he buried the baby on the mountain.
Villager II: Look. Look there!
All: Look! They are ascending into the sky on the dragon-horse's back. They are throwing down flowers. When you arrive there, please tell the highest heavenly gods that they should never send another superman to our village.
  (The singing sound of a lullaby from the sky: Our baby, a docile baby. . . .)
All: *(As if they chase the sparrows from the millet field)* Whai! Never come back again! Wha. . . i! Whai!
  (The singing sound of a lullaby from the sky: . . .
  Our baby which grows without milk. . . .)
All: Wha. . .i! Never come back again! Wha. . .i! Whai!
  (The people begin to dance as they clap their hands to the tune of farmer's music. Once in a while, they do shimmy dance as they shake their heads and shoulders.
  The singing sound of a lullaby from the sky: . . .
  Our baby which grows while fussing
  If a lean year arrives, . . .)
All: Wha. . .i! Wha. . .i! Never come back again! Wha. . .i! Whai!
  (They dance enthusiastically. They slow down their dance while the curtain is lowered.)